Teacher Wellbeing

Praise for *Teacher Wellbeing*

I absolutely loved this book. The whole thing. It is absolutely needed and so timely. This is the go-to guide for school leaders and teachers who are eager to unpack the complex issue of educator wellbeing in this current crisis and beyond. Despite the best efforts of school leaders, many of us feel that we have been falling short when it comes to understanding how to proactively attack issues such as burnout for ourselves and our staff. The chapter summaries and 'Theory into Action' learning throughout provide practical strategies for the individual and collective change that is so desperately needed for teachers and school leaders.

Celia King
School Leader

This book emphasises why teacher wellbeing is important and that it is far more than feel-good activities. Amy highlights many things that may not initially be perceived as part of wellbeing, however through explanation, research-based evidence and links to teaching, it just makes sense. Amy shows how teacher wellbeing is crucial to school culture and that we need to be open to reflecting on and changing the structures we use to support the wellbeing of teachers. This book is a must-read for leaders and teachers alike.

Dr Selena Fisk
Author, Data Storyteller

This book will resonate with many school leaders and teachers. I found myself nodding along in agreement many times. The framework Amy uses for teacher wellbeing throughout this book synthesises the elements of being and doing individually and collectively so beautifully, and fits in with all we do in schools and as humans. It aligns school culture and improvement to collective wellbeing, and in a currency of change is 100% on message and what is needed right now and beyond. It is a powerful, important, yet easy read. I struggled to put it down. I want a copy for every teacher I know.

Belinda Fenn
School Principal

Teacher Wellbeing

A Real Conversation for Teachers and Leaders

Amy Green

Copyright © Amy Green 2022

All rights reserved. No part of this book may be reproduced or transmitted in any form or by any means, electronic or mechanical, including photocopying, recording or by any information storage and retrieval system, without prior permission in writing from the publisher.

Published by Amba Press
Melbourne, Australia
www.ambapress.com.au

Editor – Brooke Lyons
Cover Designer – Tess McCabe

ISBN: 9781922607386 (pbk)
ISBN: 9781922607393 (ebk)

A catalogue record for this book is available from the National Library of Australia.

Contents

Preface: A Note to Teachers		1
Introduction		3
Part 1: What is Teacher Wellbeing?		11
1	What is Wellbeing?	15
2	The Purpose of Teacher Wellbeing	33
3	Where We Got it Wrong	53
Part 2: The Work of Wellbeing		69
4	Energy and Function	73
5	Resilience	89
6	Emotional Regulation	107
Part 3: Where to from Here?		123
7	The Power of Efficacy	127
8	What Can I Do? Practical Strategies for Teachers	145
9	What Can We Do? Practical Strategies for Schools	163
Conclusion		181
References		185
Acknowledgements		189
About the Author		191

Preface: A Note to Teachers

Hey teacher,

Firstly, thank you for picking up this book. Teacher wellbeing is a complex issue. There are things I'll talk about here that may make you smile, laugh and perhaps even cry. Be it your own wellbeing or that of your colleagues or staff, it's tricky.

While my intention with this book is to deepen our understanding of teacher wellbeing and provide practical strategies, I too want to acknowledge that there has been a lot going on lately.

This book was written post-Covid (mid 2022). Although we have learned to better live with and through the pandemic, we are still experiencing the overflow from it. If anything, Covid-19 has in some ways helped us. It has shed light on the complexities, expectations and difficulties of our profession, and amplified what was already an area of need.

The teacher shortage we knew was coming is here. The impact of the overcrowded curriculum and putting more and more pressure on teachers is here. The result of devaluing, not supporting and not appreciating our profession is here.

I'm sharing this because while I suggest strategies in this book that may not seem possible right now, or that do not acknowledge what has happened, I want you to know that I see you, I hear you and I feel you.

In writing this book I didn't set out to highlight everything that is wrong with our profession, point fingers or blame, or analyse all the issues that lie within and come from the system itself. I, like you, know these problems are there; but instead of focusing on them, I have chosen to look at what may help, what may be possible. I want to provide hope to fellow colleagues of a profession I love and am deeply passionate about. This book was not written to pull the profession down, but to give the people within it a glimmer of hope that perhaps, if we unite and support one another and are brave enough to do things differently, we might be able to change some things.

That's all I can really give any of you: the opportunity to unite together on possibility, to support each other to make change and to inspire each other to think differently. I want to give you hope.

Yes, I will give you the strategy, the knowledge, the insight, the experience and the expertise as well, but without hope, it doesn't matter.

So, teacher, I give you hope: hope that we can change what needs to be changed; hope that the system will join us, and give us the support to make it happen.

With love and kindness,

Amy

Introduction

Teaching is ingrained in me. It is part of who I am. I love it beyond words and no matter what school I am in, my passion for and commitment to helping learning improve and students thrive is at the core of all I do. That is, in part, how I ended up here.

I remember the day clearly – the day I knew something was wrong. I left school around 5 pm, drove home feeling tired and cold (it was a Canberra winter), and pulled into the underground carpark of our apartment feeling thankful I was home. I turned the car off but didn't move. I sat there. Waiting for what, I didn't know. Energy, help, to fall asleep maybe. I was exhausted, but this was also how I felt most days, so I just sat there for a few minutes, with my eyes shut, before I reached for the door handle and began unloading my bags to head upstairs.

Opening the door to my apartment would mean a whole other series of events that needed to unfold – things I felt I didn't have the energy for, but that couldn't be avoided. My cat would want to be fed, my lunch bag needed unpacking, there was housework to do and dinner to cook. I just couldn't do it. I walked in the front door, placed whatever I was holding on the kitchen bench and fell to the floor. I lay there hoping it would all go away, that I would fall asleep or that someone would rescue me.

It didn't start out like this though. My evenings had developed this pattern over time.

Most afternoons I would collapse, on the floor, half my body on the tiles and the other half stretched on the carpet, my cat usually curled up beside me or laying on my chest looking for what little affection I could give him despite my depleted energy. Lucky for him he was happy (and still is) to just be by my side.

This period of rest, unnatural to me but oh so common, could last anywhere from 20 minutes to an hour. Looking back on this, I had no idea these were the signs of exhaustion and burnout; at the time, I would have said I'd had a big day and was tired. I mean, shouldn't I be tired? I was up at 5 am and had been going all day.

Even though I was clearly showing signs of exhaustion, I had also developed a strict, fast-pace, 'doing' routine at this point of my life. Most days were as follows:

- 5 am – wake up, drink water and coffee, get my bags ready
- 5:45 am – leave for gym
- 6–7:30 am – weights and cardio
- 7:30–8 am – get ready for the day and drive to work
- 8 am–5 pm – work
- 5:30 pm – arrive home and sit in the car followed by collapsing on the floor
- 6 pm – unpack the day's bags, get organised for tomorrow
- 6:30 pm – work on my blog and side hustle at the time (somewhere in here I would eat)
- 8 pm – TV and rest
- 9 pm – bed

This was it, my average day. This routine was everything. Not only did I think it was the best thing for me, but it was also all I knew how to do. I had to keep moving; being still was not an option. I grew up in a house where you weren't allowed to sit still or you would be given something to do, and I was also a teacher – the most demanding profession there is. There was always something to do, which meant I should always be doing something. So, with these two overlapping beliefs, I managed to create an extremely busy life that started to slowly wear me down.

When I look back at that time, I can see how it all happened – how I ended up feeling worse and worse, tired, irritable and unhappy. My body was suffering. Despite being so tired, I couldn't sleep. I started taking melatonin by the double just to fall off to sleep, but would wake at 2 am or 3 am each night with eyes wide open, my mind racing, going over events from the day before and figuring out how I was going to tackle what lay ahead of me in just a few hours. This continuous and interrupted sleep pattern meant I needed coffee to start my day and keep me going through the mornings. I suffered from digestive issues and was bloated all the time, despite my obsession with counting macros and meal prepping like a pro. Friday nights felt like they did in my first year of teaching, where the thought of doing anything other than sleep seemed impossible. I broke out in cold sores (I am unlucky enough to get cold sores on my chin, nose and even inside my nose) month after month because as I learned later my cortisol was continuously running high due to my levels of exhaustion. Even my menstruation cycle was interrupted due to the high level of stress I was experiencing. You would think all these things combined would have been enough to make me realise something was wrong, but they weren't.

Not only was my body showing numerous physical signs of extreme stress, which I only recognise now I look back, but I was also irritable, cranky, found it hard to switch off, struggled to let go of things that were out of my control and obsessed over the same thoughts and ideas, which definitely wasn't good for my mental health. Again, though, I couldn't see this. It is only now looking back that I can piece it all together.

During this period in my life I loved (and still do) listening to podcasts. Several health-related podcasts were in my regular rotation at that time. One morning I found myself listening to a podcast discussing stress, what it does to the body and hormones, and how these symptoms can manifest in our bodies. Feeling bloated, not sleeping through the night, being irritable – it was my list. In the episode it was recommended that if you were experiencing these symptoms, an integrative GP may be able to help. At the time I had never heard of an integrative GP, so I asked a friend in the wellness space who was able to recommend an amazing integrative GP, who sounded exactly like what I needed.

I have been to many GPs in my life and while I got great support, I never felt like I truly understood what was going on with me. However, the integrative GP changed my life. She looked at both my physical and emotional symptoms, did extensive blood work and a cortisol test (one where I needed to spit into a jar for multiple days in a row) and just talked to me. All I could say to begin with was, 'I don't know what's wrong with me. I am tired all the time but can't sleep, and I don't feel like myself. I am usually more relaxed, calm and fun, but at the moment everything's hard. I don't like feeling like this, but I don't know what to do.'

From here we unpacked every part of my life, from work to my relationship, my exercise and training, my sleep and what I ate – everything! Slowly, with all this information and the results from multiple tests, we landed on two things. Firstly, I was living out of alignment with my values, and this was very much contributing to both my physical, mental and emotional symptoms. Secondly, I was suffering from chronic stress and burnout.

For someone like me, who I and many others saw as healthy and having it all together, this didn't seem believable. 'How could this be? How did this happen? I am not stressed; surely I am just tired.'

I was wrong. I wasn't just tired. I had, over a long time, been experiencing multiple layers of stress, both physical and emotional, some within my control and some out of my control – and my body had enough.

It was in this moment I knew I had to make a change. With the guidance of my integrative GP I devised a plan. Most significant was giving up my weight training, which I had been doing almost every day for more than seven years. The recommendation was not to reassess what I did, or what I wanted to do, but to connect me back to how I wanted to *feel*. For a long time I had simply been going through the motions of what I thought I needed to be doing to be 'successful' and 'have it all together'. Up until this point, I had never really stopped to ask myself how I wanted to feel. I was simply too busy *doing* to consider or connect with what and how I wanted to feel.

Deep down though I knew how I wanted to feel. It didn't take me long to acknowledge that I wanted to feel calm, light, fun and energised again. I wanted to be less serious, be okay with not having a tidy house all the time (I used to be obsessive about this). I didn't want to worry if I had overeaten my protein or carbohydrate intake for the day (I am proud to say I am so past this point – I haven't counted macros or calories for over a year now, which is a big deal for me). It was by adopting this way of thinking that I realised so much of what I thought was good for me was doing me damage. I had to let some things go.

This wasn't easy. It wasn't just giving up these things that I struggled with, it was letting go of who I thought I was and trying to figure out who I wanted to be in the process. I was someone who lifted weights, I was someone who counted macros, I was someone who lived to a schedule, I was someone who wouldn't stop until everything was done to my standards, I was someone who was all about being busy. I thrived off all these things; however, they were also slowly breaking me down and I knew I had to let them go.

I switched my weight training and daily cardio sessions for a more play-based style of training and joined a gym where we did things like headstands, dancing and yoga. Here I learned to laugh, play and slow down again. I worked with a nutrition coach to learn what foods worked for me, and how to eat more intuitively and still get all the nutrients that I needed. I sought out (or rather went back to) a mindset coach for some one-on-one sessions, and joined a mastermind group coaching program to help me do the internal work I needed to. I also began a daily meditation practice. All of these things combined helped me to heal, but it wasn't quick or easy: it was slow, uncomfortable and at times required a lot of effort.

This transition period took a long time. Even now I still struggle with some things; in fact I am constantly working on what I need to change and how. The only difference is I don't have to wait until I have chronic levels of stress or need to seek professional help before I do the work. I am now able to recognise the signs early. Many of the changes I made were not band-aid solutions – they became part of who I am, and I still do them today. This was the first insight I had into living based on how I wanted to feel, not just what I thought I should do. It was where my life really changed.

What's ironic is that I had started working in the wellbeing space with educators and others long before this. I worked with them on things like time management, setting boundaries and building self-care plans. I was great (and still am) at systemising these things, which is partly how I ended up where I am. However, I had too many systems based on *doing*, and none based on *feeling*.

I have spent years now compiling my thoughts and beliefs on wellbeing. Having experienced what I've shared here and more, completed study and formal training and seen various approaches in schools, I can confidently say the wellbeing work we need is not a system, schedule or checklist. It is in who we are, how we feel and who we want to be.

If I had known this, or if someone had taken the time early on to ask, really ask, and help me look at what may be impacting my current state, maybe I wouldn't have told myself that taking 20 to 45 minutes each evening to lay on the kitchen floor, too exhausted to move, was normal because 'I was a teacher, a school leader, and just tired'. Or maybe I was supposed to experience this, so I could share what I've learned with you – with all teachers who sit in the car summoning all their energy to open the door; who collapse on the floor because everything else is too hard; or who lie awake at 2 am, no matter how tired they are, without realising their body is telling them it's all too much – that this is not okay, not normal, no matter how 'tired' you are. Maybe this happened to me because I needed to be the one to share with you that there are ways to heal, to do things differently, to feel different – and that you can do this while continuing to teach and love the job that you do without feeling the stress, burnout and exhaustion.

My story is just that – a story. It is no longer what I experience, but I included it because I know it will resonate with many of you. You might be experiencing something similar right now, or perhaps in the past. Either way, experiences like these are not nice. However, once you make it to the other side (and you will), once you heal, once you find the courage to talk about it, you will help others. That is what I hope this book does: help you, every teacher and every school know that the stress and burnout teachers are experiencing right now is not okay. We all play a part in writing a better story.

The opportunity for change is within us. When we have awareness, knowledge and understanding, we can begin to make the necessary long-term sustainable changes. We can move beyond the band-aid solutions that are currently being offered and begin to realise what works for us and what matters most. This may be taking time for meditation, exercise and food preparation; it may be having the courage to initiate vulnerable conversations; or it may be strengthening your ability to say no without feeling guilty. Whatever it is, in these pages you will find a deeper, richer, more holistic approach to improving your wellbeing and that of others. It is going to be a real and honest conversation – one that requires openness, trust and compassion for self and others. This book sets out to change the way you understand your own wellbeing, what you can control and change, what you need to let go, and what you need to feel, be and do. Ultimately, though, every teacher and leader needs to have this conversation with themselves and others if we are serious about shifting the way we view teacher wellbeing. We must show teachers we value them and are serious about doing the work and enabling it to occur.

I hope this book provides you with some answers. I hope it helps you understand that you are not alone, that you matter and that you are powerful. No longer do you have to say yes to everything; no longer do you have to wear burnout as a badge; no longer should the staffroom be a place where we normalise being tired, stressed or overwhelmed.

Instead, we need to gather to celebrate the wins, collaborate on the issues at hand and remain solutions-focused when it feels all too much. We need to support each other to find new ways of doing things; hold each other to higher standards of behaviour; work together to lessen the load, especially when we know it is intense; and check in with each other to make sure we really are okay. Mostly, though, we need to ask 'How are you?' and be open to receiving an answer that we may find uncomfortable. We need to create spaces and environments where this can be done without shame, judgement or being met with dismissive comments. We need safe spaces for the work of wellbeing to occur.

Teacher wellbeing is community work. It reflects the community in which every teacher belongs: it is the students they teach, the colleagues they work with and the whole school community.

Teacher wellbeing, along with student wellbeing and the wellbeing of the wider school community, is the most significant contributor to school culture. It is the missing link in school improvement. It should be on every school improvement plan, strategic plan and budget proposal. If we want thriving cultures in our schools we have to come back to our teachers. It isn't about the lessons, the content or the assessment schedule. It's about the teachers who stand in front of students and impart so much more than knowledge. It is about who and how our teachers are. If we want real change in schools, from an individual to a systemic level, we have to get real about putting teachers at the centre of school and system-level improvement agendas.

As we know, though, that is a bigger conversation than this book – but it is not to be forgotten as you read what's to come. While each teacher or individual can do their piece, if we are serious about long-term, systemic, embedded change it must also be supported by the system as a whole.

For now, though, we can start to make changes where we are, as teachers, leaders and people who care about education. We can do the work, right here, right now. If we all work together on this, we can create change, we can influence and impact those around and above us and we can bring about transformation far beyond what we imagine.

Don't underestimate your ability to create ripples; even if you can't see them, they are there.

Note: throughout this book I will use the terms 'teacher' and 'school'. Please change these terms to suit your setting. For example, 'teacher' can mean educator, staff, leader or principal, and 'school' can mean leadership team, pre-school, kindergarten or early learning centre, wellbeing team or the people responsible for making the decisions in this space.

Part 1

What is Teacher Wellbeing?

Wellbeing is easier defined and understood in a broader context, with teacher wellbeing being a relatively new and unknown field. While teacher wellbeing has always been important, it hasn't always been an agenda item for a staff meeting, appeared on school improvement plans or been the theme of educational conferences like it is now. Teachers have always known it is needed, and now those in the space of influence are starting to make it matter – and, to be honest, it is about time.

In Part 1 we'll explore three important topics we need to understand before we can get to work on improving teacher wellbeing:
- what is wellbeing?
- the purpose of teacher wellbeing
- where we got it wrong.

Teacher wellbeing is about valuing and recognising the incredible work teachers do, while ensuring they can work and function at their best. If we don't understand what wellbeing is, why we need to focus on it or how to prioritise it, while recognising where we have gone wrong so far, we have very little chance of making long-term change. I believe that part of the issue with defining and understanding teacher wellbeing is the urgency we feel around *doing* something about it, as opposed to really understanding what it is and why it is so important.

I have met with many school leaders, wellbeing teams and teachers to discuss teacher wellbeing. Many of these conversations were centred around what was happening at their school, what they noticed about their staff and what their significant concerns were. For the most part, these discussions flowed easily, and the people I was speaking with could clearly articulate the behaviours and feelings they noticed in themselves and their staff. What often surprised me, though, was that no matter how easily teachers and leaders were able to share the challenges around teacher wellbeing, they weren't able to follow up with what they believed optimal wellbeing would look like for themselves or their staff.

While we all want to be less stressed and overwhelmed, happy, organised, working well together and productive, these terms can differ in meaning from person to person and be tricky to measure. For teacher wellbeing to become a priority, and to be easily and practically addressed, we must be far more specific with how we think about, describe, explain and set expectations around the change we would like to see. If we are to truly understand what teacher wellbeing is, and have an impact in this space, we need to know what we are trying to achieve.

The same can be said for individual teacher wellbeing. It is easy to list off the many gripes that come with the profession, the things that are frustrating and causing stress and overwhelm; but unless we know how we want to feel and be, and can describe the changes we are longing for, it's hard to know what to change or improve.

This is important to note. Our inability to be clear about what teacher wellbeing is, either for ourselves or our staff, might be what is getting in the way of making the changes we are so hungry for. We all need to commit to being clear on what wellbeing is, what we want to change and how we want it to look. We must prioritise the work of teacher wellbeing and come together to make the changes we agree on.

While we may never have a universal definition for teacher wellbeing, I encourage you as you read the following chapters to begin considering what *your* definition of wellbeing is. It is essential that each school and/or system defines teacher wellbeing clearly and consistently. This will allow leaders, wellbeing teams and teachers to better collect data, measure, reflect and change the approaches and strategies they are implementing for themselves or their staff.

In the next few chapters I will unpack how we might define teacher wellbeing, talk you through ways to prioritise it while not losing sight of school or professional goals, and highlight some errors we have made along the way and how we can begin to improve these.

As you read the next few chapters and begin to tackle this new approach, keep in mind that the definition and actions of wellbeing are not the same for all, which means there may be differences for the individuals and groups you connect with. While I am not sure this can be avoided (and perhaps it shouldn't be), I do think if we are able to define teacher wellbeing at an individual and collective level, are consistent in schools, and agree that teacher wellbeing is part of employee wellbeing which encompasses both everyday and workplace wellbeing, we will be in a far better position to create long-term, sustainable change.

I have no doubt that the next few chapters will make you think, question and ponder your own approaches to teacher wellbeing or those of the school you work in. This is a good thing. As Henry Ford said, 'If you always do what you've always done, you will always get what you've always got.' I'm sure you will agree that we can no longer do what we have always done.

So, let's dive in. Together let's unlearn and relearn some significant pieces of knowledge, so teacher wellbeing is no longer just about what teachers do, but who they are, how they feel and the connection between their own wellbeing and learning and teaching.

Chapter 1

What is Wellbeing?

*Life has no meaning.
Each of us has meaning and we bring it to life.
It is a waste to be asking the question when you are the answer.*
– Joseph Campbell

Wellbeing is far more complex than what most of us understand it to be. It is also far more complex than the simple strategies or activities we use to try to solve the issue. A deeper understanding of what wellbeing is, how it looks for individuals, teams and schools, and how it can be approached is needed to create the change we all know we need.

Wellbeing is not something that can be summed up in one sentence, nor can it be solved with a one-size-fits-all solution. That's why there is a substantial range of wellbeing definitions to choose from. Have you ever typed into your search engine, 'What is the definition of wellbeing?' If you have, you will know there are a multitude of people and organisations out there trying to synthesise wellbeing into a simple, easy-to-understand definition – sometimes with a matching graphic or framework.

However, multilayered and dimensional aspects of our personal and workplace wellbeing can't always be divided into eight equal parts that are easy to demonstrate on a pie chart, nor can they be represented through a self-care checklist or framework that implies you must 'do one of these five things to improve your wellbeing'. Wellbeing is just not that simple.

Table 1 lists just some of the definitions of wellbeing. With dictionaries offering different definitions, it is no wonder many of us are scratching our heads wondering exactly what wellbeing is, and what we should do about it.

Source	Definition
Cambridge Dictionary (Cambridge University Press 2022)	'The state of feeling healthy and happy.'
Better Health Channel (2021)	'Wellbeing is not just the absence of disease or illness. It's a complex combination of a person's physical, mental, emotional and social health factors. Wellbeing is strongly linked to happiness and life satisfaction. In short, wellbeing could be described as how you feel about yourself and your life.'
Collins Dictionary (Collins 2022)	'The condition of being contented, healthy, or successful; welfare.'
Be You/Beyond Blue (2022)	'Wellbeing encompasses the health of the whole person – physical, mental, social and emotional. A person's wellbeing can change moment to moment, day to day, month to month and year to year. It can be influenced by what's happening in a specific moment and the actions that people take.'
Australian Curriculum, Assessment and Reporting Authority (ACARA; n.d.)	'A sense of satisfaction, happiness, effective social functioning and spiritual health, and dispositions of optimism, openness, curiosity and resilience.'

Table 1: Definitions of Wellbeing

Mental Health: A State of Wellbeing

Through my research and studies in positive psychology and wellbeing, there are two approaches to wellbeing that I put at the top of my list. The first is from the World Health Organization (WHO). The WHO Constitution (World Health Organization 2022a) says 'Health is a state of complete physical, mental and social well-being and not merely the absence of disease or infirmity.' It describes mental health as follows, and within this defines wellbeing (I encourage you to read this through a few times):

> *Mental health is a state of well-being in which an individual realizes his or her own abilities, can cope with the normal stresses of life, can work productively and is able to make a contribution to his or her community.*
>
> *Mental health is fundamental to our collective and individual ability as humans to think, emote, interact with each other, earn a living and enjoy life. On this basis, the promotion, protection and restoration of mental health can be regarded as a vital concern. (World Health Organization 2022b)*

According to the WHO, mental health is a state of wellbeing. This means when we talk about improving teacher wellbeing, what we are also trying to improve is the mental health of our teachers. Mental health seems to have a far more serious tone to it than wellbeing, yet according to the WHO, one does not exist without the other. If this is true, then perhaps wellbeing is far more significant than the inspirational quotes on staffroom walls or ad-hoc social events we so often see.

By unpacking the WHO definition, we can begin to see just how complex wellbeing is. Let's break it down.

Health is:
- a state of complete physical, mental and social wellbeing
- not merely the absence of disease or infirmity.

Mental health is a state of wellbeing in which a person:
- realises their own abilities
- can cope with the normal stresses of life
- can work productively
- can contribute to their community.

To contextualise this definition, it is helpful to break it down further and relate it to teaching and life as a teacher. As a teacher, it means:
- understanding wellbeing is firstly a balance of our physical, mental and social wellbeing and that we need to actively look after and prioritise each
- knowing our wellbeing should be a priority all the time, not just as a way to heal from or overcome mental illness or disorders
- recognising our own abilities, strengths and the things in which we find enjoyment and energy, and being able to bring this to the work space
- being able to cope with normal stresses of teacher life – for example, the start of a new school year, report-writing times, assessment-heavy periods and end-of-year concerts – and life outside school
- being productive: getting things done in a timely manner, adhering to timeframes and completing tasks to a high standard, without overworking or burning out
- contributing to the community, which may mean the school community or a community outside of school.

Wellbeing is not just activities we do or knowing that we aren't unwell or experiencing mental disorders; it's how we recognise and honour our strengths, whether we can manage the day-to-day stresses of life and teaching, and whether we are productive both in and out of the classroom and contributing beyond ourselves. Optimal wellbeing is essential for us to be able to think, problem-solve, create, connect, contribute, teach, work and live life in a fulfilling and meaningful way. This means it is essential for us to do our job well, to feel happy and enjoy life both as a teacher and as a person.

If we don't actively look after our wellbeing, we can't possibly teach to the best of our ability. We can't plan great lessons, we can't connect with our students and we can't collaborate or support our colleagues. Instead, we are just coping, trying to survive; we're waiting for the bell to ring, for it to be Friday or the end of term. When we are in this state of mind, we aren't enjoying life, we aren't able to manage the day-to-day stresses of work and life, and our mental health is impacted.

After breaking wellbeing down into these areas, I can understand and sympathise when teachers share that their school doesn't look after their wellbeing, or that they are sick of hearing how they just need to 'walk it off' or 'go to bed earlier'. Wellbeing is about how we manage all aspects of teaching – physical, mental and social. It is about how we feel long-term. It's about the tools and strategies we use and build upon that allow us to better realise and step into our own abilities, cope with normal teacher stress, be productive at our jobs and within other areas of life and contribute beyond ourselves. It is so much more than a morning tea.

I want you to think for a minute: are the strategies in your school to support wellbeing designed to be long-term, sustainable solutions, adapted for the individual? Or are they reactive, quick-fix, one-size-fits-all approaches? Do the strategies focus on improving physical, mental and social wellbeing, or do they centre more around opportunities for social events? Do they promote ways to better manage stress, be productive and work to your strengths? Do they allow you to contribute to the community, or do they take time away from doing what is really needed?

You are not alone if you realise your current approaches to wellbeing are less than optimal. I have seen many schools try things such as getting a yoga teacher in, putting a fruit bowl on the staffroom table, regularly offering morning teas and scheduling meeting-free weeks. While a lack of understanding of the definition of wellbeing is partly to blame for this, so is the approach to wellbeing we commonly see that is more about self-care. Not only is it common to see quick-fix, self-care solutions proposed as a way to fix wellbeing, it is also preferred by most and what many are looking for – despite these band-aid solutions leaving many with the same problems: not enough time or energy, feeling stressed and overwhelmed and not feeling any more organised or productive.

A better understanding of wellbeing opens a whole new realm of possibilities for what a wellbeing approach and strategy may look like for teachers, staff, teams, leaders and schools. We need to shift our understanding of wellbeing – what we think we need, what we ask for from our leaders or school and what we expect to see when wellbeing becomes a priority and changes are made. Wellbeing as a part of cultural change most likely won't look as everyone wants it to look. It requires more work, more vulnerability and more responsibility than a yoga class or team bushwalk.

Breaking down our understanding of wellbeing and being open to realising that there is a distinct difference between wellbeing and self-care will allow us to be more intentional with the strategies we implement. Wellbeing is who we are and how we feel. It's improved by long-term, sustainable strategies. Wellbeing doesn't have an end point; it continually evolves, shifts and changes depending on our circumstances, the environment, other people and our knowledge and understanding. Yet many of us, individually and as schools, wellbeing committees and teaching teams, lack an understanding of what true wellbeing is and the different ways in which wellbeing needs to be approached. Many are still looking for one-size-fits-all quick fixes that continually let us down. It is time this ends.

Subjective and Psychological Wellbeing

Now that we have a better understanding of wellbeing from the WHO, we can see its complexities and understand that we need to broaden both our understanding and approach to teacher wellbeing. Let's begin this by exploring subjective and psychological wellbeing.

It's argued (and this is still up for debate) that there are two separate yet related areas of wellbeing. The first is subjective (hedonic) wellbeing, and the second is psychological (eudaimonic) wellbeing. I have found that looking at wellbeing through these two lenses allows us to build better strategies, and focus on ways to build our everyday wellbeing and workplace wellbeing.

Ryan and Deci (2021) describe subjective (hedonic) wellbeing in terms of pleasure attainment and pain avoidance. They say the subjective approach focuses on happiness. The psychological (eudaimonic) approach, on the other hand, focuses on meaning and self-realisation, and whether a person is fully functioning (see figure 1). Subjective wellbeing is most commonly external to us – a quick fix that brings instant positive feelings and is pleasure-driven and easy; whereas psychological wellbeing focuses on more complex, internally based ideas such as meaning, fulfilment, connection and growth.

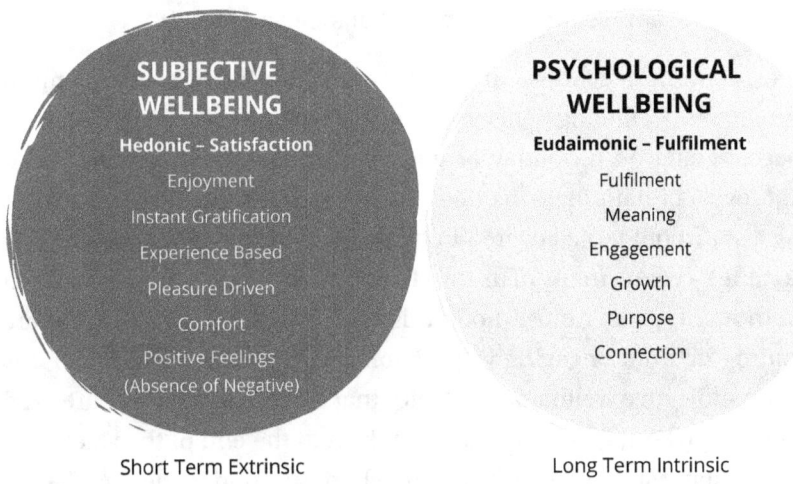

Figure 1: Subjective and Psychological Wellbeing

When it comes to teachers, it must be acknowledged that both subjective and psychological wellbeing are as important as one another – they both equally contribute to an individual's wellbeing. At the moment, though, our balance between the two is slightly off.

Subjective wellbeing has, for some time, been the main focus of improving teacher wellbeing. It is the pursuit of happiness and a pleasant life that has led to many of us relying too much on the quick-fix, feel-good approaches (also known as self-care) that we often see in schools as a means to improve wellbeing – when perhaps we would find meaningful, long-term change if we also focused on the components that make up psychological wellbeing.

Self-care has become evident and popular as a wellbeing strategy, because we have come to believe that we should 'just do what makes us happy'. However, when looking at subjective and psychological wellbeing, it's clear we have to go beyond the pursuit of happiness, knowing that wellbeing also means the ability to face challenges. What if, instead of opting for a feel-good morning tea, we had a conversation about the level of fulfilment each of us feel in our role and what we feel may be lacking for us? One focuses on the hedonic (morning teas make us feel good/happy, even if for a fleeting moment) and one focuses on the eudemonic (the conversation about fulfilment). We have to be prepared to tackle both aspects of our wellbeing to have a balanced approach.

It is evident that schools and teachers have been overly focused on subjective wellbeing. This may be partly because things such as massages, going on a holiday or getting a manicure contribute to our instant levels of happiness, as does having a staff meeting cancelled or seeing a staffroom table covered in treats for morning tea. However, it is these things – which many of us turn to on a daily or weekly basis without much thought, apart from 'I hope this makes me feel better' – that are preventing us from engaging in psychological wellbeing solutions. It is often the subjective wellbeing strategies that we turn to when we are tired and need a pick-me-up, or when we make it to the end of the week. It is also what many school leaders turn to when they notice their staff are a little flat, are working harder than usual, or when reports are due. In the fleeting moment, it works, but the pleasure of a chocolate bar does not outlast well-ingrained feelings of overwhelm or stress.

As much as we prioritise and focus on our subjective wellbeing, so too must we prioritise and focus on our psychological wellbeing. Psychological wellbeing is the piece we have been missing when it comes to improving teacher wellbeing. As we know, we do subjective wellbeing quite well – most likely because it is easy to organise, it is external to us, it makes us feel instantly good, it gives us fleeting moments of happiness, and if we don't know what to do we can jump online and find a checklist of '20 different ways to improve wellbeing'. Our psychological wellbeing is worthy of just as much time, energy and commitment; however, it is far more complex and requires a different approach. Ryff and Keys (1995) refer to six key dimensions of wellness in their theoretical approach to psychological wellbeing: self-acceptance, positive relationships, autonomy, environmental mastery, purpose in life and personal growth (see table 2).

Psychological Dimension	Determining Factors
Self-acceptance	• Positive attitude towards self • Acknowledging and accepting positive and not-so-positive qualities • Positive feelings about the past
Positive relations with others	• Warm, satisfying, trusting relationships • Concern for the welfare of others • Capacity for empathy, affection and intimacy • Understanding of give-and-take
Autonomy	• Self-determination and independence • Ability to resist social pressure • Capacity to regulate behaviour • Self-evaluation based on personal values
Environmental mastery	• Sense of mastery and competence • Ability to control activities and leverage opportunities • Capacity to choose or create contexts that suit needs and values
Purpose in life	• Having goals and a sense of direction • Feeling there is meaning to present and past life • Believing in life purpose and objectives for living
Personal growth	• Sense that you are growing and expanding • Open to new experiences • Realisation of your potential • Change that reflects greater self-knowledge

Table 2: Six Dimensions of Wellness
(Source: Adapted from Celestine 2021a)

These six key dimensions help us to see that, while subjective wellbeing can help us to feel happy in the moment and boost our mood, long-term psychological strategies aren't as quick, easy or at times as fun. That said, they are still very important.

When we begin to think about wellbeing as not just what we do to make sure we are happy all the time, or to pick us up when we feel down, but as something that is linked to fulfilment, purpose, connection and growth, it opens up a whole new way to approach the work we need to do both as teachers, and in schools as a collective. It allows us to not only focus on what we do, but also who we are, who we want to be, how we feel and how we want to feel and be in the future. With this comes a different way of thinking about, planning for and working towards improving our wellbeing. Gone is the idea that we should just tick a few things off a list like get a mani/pedi and go to yoga, or have a weekly morning tea; instead, we realise that the work of wellbeing is happening all the time. It exists in our thinking, our conversations, the people we connect with, how we spend our time, what we belong to, what we focus on and the deliberate, intentional daily decisions we make and actions we take. It also links to how we operate in our school, plan, teach, organise our day, work in teams, collaborate, make decisions, and reflect and improve our practice.

A Framework for Teacher Wellbeing

Now we have a better understanding of wellbeing as a whole and can see how complex it really is, it's clear that we need a more thorough and relatable framework that supports teacher wellbeing both in and out of the classroom.

While there are a number of frameworks, approaches, definitions and ways to 'do' wellbeing, we need something that works and is contextual for us as teachers. The definition we use for teacher wellbeing needs to be aligned with what we need to live well and teach well. It needs to work for our everyday and workplace wellbeing, and support the point of need for each teacher, team and school.

Every teacher, team and school needs to have autonomy over their definition of wellbeing, so that it can be adapted to their context. We need to promote a balanced approach, that supports both quality of life and our ability to function positively, while also acknowledging the ups and downs that occur.

We have to acknowledge too that wellbeing is not about being happy all the time or thinking there is something wrong with us should we not feel happy. Happiness is a state we feel when something positive has happened or is happening to us. Happiness is also linked to other emotions such as joy, contentment, satisfaction, gratitude, excitement or even pride. We can be both happy and sad at the same time. If this is the case, implying that wellbeing relies solely on being happy suggests that all other emotions are invalid when it comes to being in an optimal and flourishing state of wellbeing. As you will discover when we look at emotional regulation as part of everyday wellbeing, all emotions are valid and play a key part in our wellbeing.

Being flexible with our definition of wellbeing and knowing it may look different from person to person, team to team or school to school adds to the complexity of a topic we are determined to simplify. However, the only way we can simplify something as complex as wellbeing is to be open to the fact that it looks different in each scenario.

When creating a framework for teacher wellbeing, I researched and took inspiration from many; but ultimately I kept coming back to wanting an approach or framework that was underpinned by positive psychology, including both subjective and psychological wellbeing, and that would support teacher wellbeing both in and out of the classroom. I am a teacher; I know how challenging the job is and what it involves. I know what it is like to struggle to identify with anything but being a teacher, to struggle to have a life both in and out of the classroom, and to experience overwhelm and occupational stress and burnout, and then make it to the other side. Taking all this into consideration, let me introduce to you the 'Teacher Wellbeing Framework for Everyday and Workplace Wellbeing' (figure 2 overleaf).

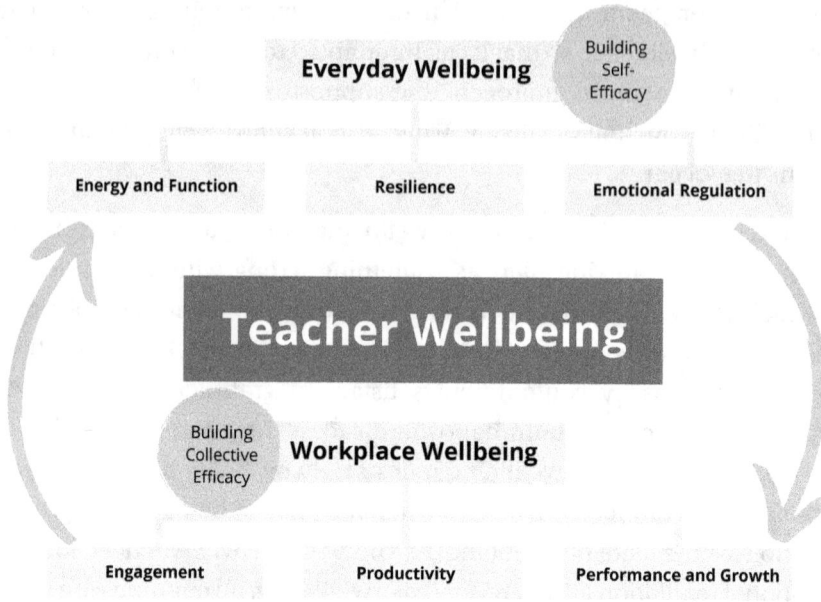

Figure 2: Teacher Wellbeing Framework for Everyday and Workplace Wellbeing

What you see here is a framework that:
- allows you define wellbeing your way
- supports you both in and out of the classroom
- acknowledges the overlap between person and teacher through everyday and workplace wellbeing
- supports subjective and psychological wellbeing
- empowers teachers and schools to work alongside each other on aligned strategies
- develops a shared language for teacher wellbeing.

You'll see this framework is split into two main areas: everyday and workplace wellbeing. Each component of wellbeing has three main sub-areas which support subjective and psychological wellbeing and help to improve teacher wellbeing both in and out of the classroom.

Everyday wellbeing centres around how you feel: your energy levels and ability to function, your resilience, and emotional regulation. Workplace wellbeing focuses on engagement, productivity and performance and growth. Each allows schools and teachers to develop their own approaches to wellbeing and build collective approaches where needed. Through a shared understanding of what wellbeing is, consistent language and a collective approach, working on wellbeing as teachers and schools using this framework becomes simplified, manageable and adaptable to each individual's need.

What is Wellbeing to You?

As shown in this chapter, there is no one answer to the question 'What is wellbeing?'. There's no one framework, no singular definition and no one-size-fits-all approach. Experts in this field have been studying wellbeing for years, and still can't agree on one definition. That's why wellbeing is tough to pinpoint: it flows and changes, spins and twirls, never still or stagnant.

We don't necessarily need a definition of wellbeing straight away to be able to work on it; we just need to be able to agree that it matters, and that how we go about it may need to change. There is no one right answer, or one right way.

If you were to ask me to define wellbeing, I wouldn't be able to answer with one sentence, either. It is too complex for that. What I can tell you though is what it feels like to have suboptimal wellbeing – I know the sluggish feeling when my energy is low, and how hard it is at times to function when I'm in this state. I can tell you that my energy levels impact my ability to think, and my ability to use resilience strategies that support me instead of pull me down. I can also tell you that when this happens my ability to regulate my emotions is not good. You see, all components of our everyday wellbeing are related and connected. Therefore, we need to focus on all elements to achieve an optimal and flourishing state.

The same can be said for workplace wellbeing. If we aren't doing what we need to do to have optimal energy, like sleeping or eating the right foods, we are going to struggle with all aspects of our workplace wellbeing. We can't be productive when we are tired, perform or grow if we have limited energy, work cohesively or collaborate if we can't regulate our emotions.

We can't overcome the daily stresses of teaching or be engaged in our work if we don't know about resilience strategies that support us or how to use them. It all goes together and as teachers, we need to make sure we are building our capacity to know what wellbeing is to us.

So, instead of looking for a singular definition of wellbeing, ask yourself this: 'What is wellbeing to me?'

You get to decide what wellbeing is for you, what your version of 'optimal wellbeing' is, and what areas you want to develop or grow in. You don't have to wait for someone to give you a framework, to tell you how it is going to be, what is important for your wellbeing, or what you need to do – you get to decide.

Chapter Summary

- There are multiple definitions for wellbeing.
- Wellbeing is not easily defined and needs to be contextualised to the person or setting.
- Wellbeing is not a one-size-fits-all approach.
- Wellbeing requires a balance of subjective and psychological approaches.
- We need to focus on how we want to feel and be, not just what we do.

From Theory to Action

What is Wellbeing to Me?

Now that you understand what wellbeing is, despite its complexities, one of the most powerful things you can do is define wellbeing for yourself using both the WHO and subjective and psychological approaches.

First, let's start with breaking down the WHO definition. Use each of the statements below to help you break down this definition and begin to create your own.

Part 1: My Optimal Health

My physical health is in an optimal state when:	
My mental health is in an optimal state when:	
My social health is in an optimal state when:	

Part 2: My State of Wellbeing

I know my own abilities; these include:	
Normal stress I cope with includes:	
I work productively when:	
I contribute to my community by:	

Once you have jotted some ideas down, you can begin to use these to formulate your own individual definition of wellbeing. For example, 'I know I am in optimal physical health when …'; 'Being in optimal mental health means I …'

Upon completing this, it is important too that we each respect and understand everyone's unique wellbeing journey and that people will be at different places, choose to focus on different things and want to achieve different results. This is why wellbeing is not a one-size fits-all approach – why we can't give everyone the same checklist to complete or keep focusing on the subjective wellbeing area only. It's all areas, all at once and is different for everyone.

My Ideal Average Day

Not long after I began studying human behaviour I was introduced to the concept that I get to decide how my day looks, how I want to feel, and who I want to be. I learned about the following activity from The Coaching Institute and Sharon Pearson.

The activity asks you to design your ideal average day. When this was first introduced to me it didn't occur to me that I could be an active participant in the design of my day. I realised that for a really long time I had been on autopilot – going through the motions from A to B, doing what I thought I 'should', as opposed to what I really wanted. This was perhaps my first insight into designing my own wellbeing strategy (although at the time I didn't realise it).

I remember doing this activity, sometime in 2014 I think, and it has always stuck with me as something everyone should do. In some way, this is your definition of wellbeing in action. How you want to be, who you want to be, how you want to feel, what you want to do, what you want to experience – this is what matters to your wellbeing. It involves recognising that it is the small things in our day that we need to focus on and build intentionally, instead of focusing on what we don't want, the mundane or what is in our way.

The idea is to keep it simple; to find peace in the simple things that we can do well, easily and with joy. Enjoy this activity, come back to it as often as you need, daydream and let your imagination run wild in the possibilities that will allow you to design not just your average day, but your definition of wellbeing too.

Thinking of your ideal average day, answer the following questions:
- How do you feel when you wake up?
- Where are you?
- What is the first thing you do?
- What do you have for breakfast?
- Where do you work?
- What do you do during the day?
- Who do you speak with?
- What sorts of conversations do you have?
- What brings you joy throughout the work day?
- What do you do after work?
- How do you spend your evening?
- What do you do to wind down?
- How do you feel before bed?

What about a bit more long-term? (This might be over a month as opposed to a day.)
- What fulfils you each day?
- How do you continue to grow?
- What is your purpose? How do you achieve this?

Remember, this task is to help you achieve your ideal average day, not a day on holidays, or as if you have won the lotto.

Chapter 2

The Purpose of Teacher Wellbeing

The best thing about being a teacher is that it matters.
The hardest thing about being a teacher is that it matters every day.
– Todd Whitaker

Teachers matter. They are the heart of each school, the engines, the worker bees. They keep everything pumping, turning and working. Without our teachers, there wouldn't be schools, but more importantly, there wouldn't be that significant person who shows up every day to care for and teach students.

While we know teachers matter, the question 'How much does teacher wellbeing matter?' is still something we are having to debate.

Teachers spend a significant number of their waking hours at school, so it makes sense that their wellbeing impacts how they teach and perform. Knowing our teachers influence so many areas of school culture, it's clear we need teachers who have flourishing wellbeing and who actively take care of their physical, mental and emotional health as well.

There are many reasons people believe we should prioritise wellbeing: it contributes to our happiness and makes life easier; it allows us to connect better with others, feel better about ourselves and manage stress more effectively; we tend to be more resilient, creative and feel more satisfied in life, and have a growth mindset; and it increases positive emotions.

When we were looking at the definition of wellbeing in Chapter 1, I introduced the idea that teacher wellbeing comprises two parts: everyday wellbeing and workplace wellbeing. This means we are not asking the wellbeing of teachers to exist outside of how they do their jobs, but for the connection between everyday wellbeing and workplace wellbeing to be understood.

In the workplace, increased employee wellbeing has a strong positive impact on how individuals and teams work. Most significantly are the wellbeing benefits that can be obtained from focusing on the following three areas: *engagement, performance* and *productivity* (Celestine 2021b). (We'll unpack these three areas in more detail later in the chapter.) These three areas are crucial to how we operate as teachers; therefore, it makes sense that they are three great reasons to work on teacher wellbeing through everyday and workplace approaches.

This does provoke a question, however: if employee wellbeing consists of both everyday and workplace wellbeing, then what is the purpose of prioritising teacher wellbeing for teachers themselves, and for schools? There are four main reasons we should prioritise teacher wellbeing, each with significant outcomes and impact (see table 3).

Reason	Outcome and Impact
To improve individual teacher wellbeing and self-efficacy.	• Teachers understand what wellbeing is and how it impacts their life both in and out of the classroom. • Teachers know their own wellbeing strategies for everyday and workplace wellbeing. • Teachers are proactive in what they need to do to look after their wellbeing. • Teachers believe they can make the changes they need to improve their wellbeing.

To improve collective teacher wellbeing and collective efficacy.	• Teachers have a shared definition of what wellbeing is and work together to support each other. • Teachers use a common language to talk about wellbeing. • Teachers collaborate and reflect on current ways of working that may be impacting wellbeing, and seek solutions where needed. • Teachers know they can make a difference in the collective space.
To enhance school culture.	• All stakeholders share the same definition and understanding of wellbeing. • Wellbeing is a key driver in decision-making. • Wellbeing is openly discussed, shared and valued. • Systems, structures and processes support everyday and workplace wellbeing.
To improve student learning and outcomes.	• Teachers are more aware of students' academic, social and emotional needs • Teachers foster better relationships with students • Teachers are more organised, well-planned and present when teaching • Teachers are more open to change and improvement.

Table 3: Why we Should Prioritise Teacher Wellbeing

Table 3 demonstrates a number of reasons why we should prioritise teacher wellbeing, however alongside knowing why this matters, we also need to ensure we make it a priority for teachers, teams and whole schools.

Prioritising teacher wellbeing means being *proactive* – not *reactive* – in our approach to managing the wellbeing of ourselves and our staff. This is the difference between ensuring we have strong systems and structures that support teacher wellbeing, rather than defaulting to yoga teachers and morning teas, or waiting until holidays to rest. By prioritising teacher wellbeing, we are aiming to prevent teachers from experiencing high stress, overwhelm and burnout, and from their profession negatively impacting their mental health.

Black Dog Institute (2022) reports that 'mental illness is now the leading cause of sickness, absence and long-term work incapacity in Australia'. Knowing this, it makes sense that schools should have a proactive teacher wellbeing approach that supports the prevention of mental illness, and that focuses on looking after, building the capacity of and retaining staff. So what does a proactive teacher wellbeing approach look like and what does it involve?

Firstly, we have to understand the reason we need to have proactive teacher wellbeing approaches is to ensure we are supporting educators to be 'fit for purpose'. While this might sound a little dry, ultimately what it means is that the wellbeing strategies we utilise in schools (workplace wellbeing) serve the purpose of helping teachers teach better. This is the reason teacher wellbeing matters. We want happy, healthy teachers on our staff, working at our schools, teaching our students. This is 'fit for purpose' teacher wellbeing, and the strategies we use here should support all areas of employee wellbeing, which includes both everyday and workplace strategies.

These strategies, or the areas a school might choose to focus on to support workplace wellbeing, lie within the systems, structures and processes that inform how a school operates. For example, things such as planning, team meetings, pedagogical approaches and assessment all require systems structures and processes to operate – which can either support or inhibit engagement, performance and growth, and productivity. Workplace wellbeing in schools also includes a school's commitment to building collective teacher efficacy, establishing cohesive and collaborative teams and having a strong and positive school culture.

So, if this is workplace wellbeing, where does everyday wellbeing fit into teacher wellbeing? Everyday wellbeing plays a key role in the wellbeing of teachers. Energy and function, resilience and emotional regulation are the three main areas of everyday wellbeing for teachers. While these do overlap with workplace wellbeing, these three areas are ultimately part of everyday wellbeing and are therefore difficult for a school to significantly impact.

In Part 2 of this book, we'll unpack energy and function, resilience and emotional regulation in more detail, but what you will find is that a lot of the strategies to support this need to be done by the individual, the teacher. However, I encourage and recommended that as part of workplace wellbeing, schools support teachers in understanding what these three areas are and commit to recognising these as factors contributing to their wellbeing. To do this, schools should also look to build their staff's professional and personal knowledge in these areas, include them in their own approach to staff wellbeing, and be mindful of systems, structures, processes and school cultures that may be impacting areas of everyday wellbeing. For example, if we have dysfunctional teams, poor communication and lack processes around planning, these things may impact teachers' emotional states, their ability to function and their resilience due to feeling continuous pressure – all which impact everyday wellbeing.

Along with everyday and workplace wellbeing, teacher wellbeing also focuses on building self-efficacy and collective efficacy. Self-efficacy is built alongside establishing strategies to support everyday wellbeing, while collective efficacy is built alongside workplace wellbeing (see figure 3 overleaf). Many of you may be familiar with the term collective efficacy and understand that it is the belief a group or team has that they can create change and have impact. Collective teacher efficacy is our ability to believe that the work we do together as teachers impacts students' outcomes. Self-efficacy is similar in that it is linked to the beliefs we hold regarding our own ability; it's the belief we have in ourselves, rather than the collective, that we can do and create the change we seek. We will further explore the concepts of self and collective efficacy and how they support teacher wellbeing in Part 3.

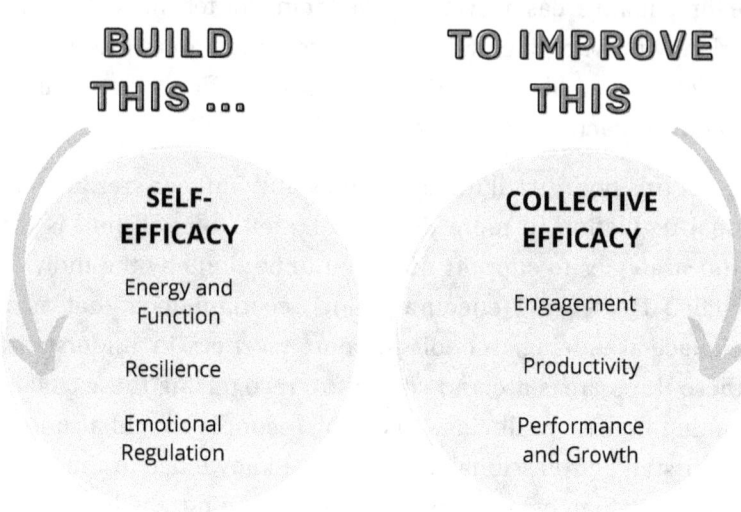

Figure 3: Self-Efficacy and Collective Efficacy

Let's now take a look at everyday wellbeing and workplace wellbeing in more detail.

Everyday Wellbeing: Energy and Function, Resilience and Emotional Regulation

Our ability to have and maintain the required level of energy and function, resilience and emotional regulation allows us to be engaged, productive and perform well. Both aspects are key to overall employee wellbeing.

However, at a school level, this is not the main area of focus. As mentioned, our wellbeing approaches need to be fit for purpose, hence everyday wellbeing focusing on energy and function, resilience, and emotional regulation and workplace wellbeing being more specific to our role as a teacher.

As this chapter is focusing on the purpose of teacher wellbeing in schools, the rest of it will be dedicated to workplace wellbeing – engagement, productivity and performance and growth. However, because I believe in valuing *people before performance,* as I do *connection before content,* the entire of Part 2 will be dedicated to everyday teacher wellbeing – specifically unpacking and supporting you to understand and build strategies for energy and function, resilience and emotional regulation. Without truly understanding your everyday wellbeing, how to look after yourself and what your own strategies are for these areas, workplace wellbeing will not be as powerful as it could be.

Engagement can't occur, productivity will be hindered and performance and growth will be low if we don't first honour our teachers and support them with their energy and function, resilience and emotional regulation. We must look after the person before focusing on the teacher – person first, teacher second.

There is a tiered approach for teacher wellbeing that can be helpful to follow (see figure 4): first everyday wellbeing (what the individual teacher needs), followed by workplace wellbeing (what, at a school level, we must prioritise and build) and lastly team wellbeing (which can only be achieved once we establish everyday and workplace wellbeing).

Figure 4: The Teacher Wellbeing Tiered Approach

Workplace Wellbeing: Engagement, Productivity and Performance and Growth

Engagement, productivity and performance and growth are indicators of high workplace wellbeing. They support the notion that one enjoys their work (engagement), works efficiently, including using time effectively (productivity), and produces work to a standard agreed upon by their employer and is always looking to improve (performance and growth). In the teaching space, this means we have teachers who enjoy their job and like coming to school, are able to complete tasks in a reasonable timeframe, who work to a standard as per school and system expectations – for example, the Australian Institute for Teaching and School Leadership (AITSL) standards – and are always reflecting and aiming to improve. Furthermore, engagement, productivity and performance and growth help to support the six dimensions of psychological wellbeing we discussed in Chapter 1.

Each of these three areas also feed into each other: building employee engagement helps to create a positive workplace culture that drives productivity and in return improves performance. This again emphasises that when we prioritise teacher wellbeing, it is not something that is done without considering how we are ensuring we are 'fit for purpose', or without coming back to teacher wellbeing supporting how we feel and how we work.

Let's now take a look at each of the three elements of workplace wellbeing in more detail.

Engagement

'If we can improve teacher engagement we will improve student outcomes.' Have you heard this before? Yep, me too. Many who try to tackle engagement come at it from the angle of why it serves students. While this is important, what if we instead looked at engagement as a way to improve and serve the wellbeing of *teachers*? Knowing that engagement is the first component of workplace wellbeing, it would pay to do this well. Engagement in our work is related to job satisfaction, which in return influences things such as productivity, collaboration, performance and growth, and retention and attrition. So how do we ensure teacher engagement is teacher driven, not only student driven?

Engagement is connected to a number of areas in psychological wellbeing that also influence workplace wellbeing and job satisfaction. Autonomy, positive relationships with others and personal growth are linked to engagement, and for many, *purpose* is also a key contributing factor to their overall workplace wellbeing. Making sure we allow for these areas of psychological wellbeing to be met through engagement (as well as other areas) ensures we are building the foundations for workplace wellbeing for teachers, from which everything else can follow on.

Like many other aspects of wellbeing, engagement varies in definition and behaviour from person to person. High engagement for one person may look different to another based on how people externally and internally operate. Here are some of the ways engagement has been described:

- 'Individuals' commitment to their work, their satisfaction from their work and the enthusiasm they feel about their work' (Robbins and Judge 2012).
- 'A positive behavior or a state of mind that leads to positive results in the work. Work engagement is defined as effective and positive cognitive state, vigor, commitment, and absorption' (Roozeboom and Schelvis 2015).
- 'When people express themselves physically, cognitively and mentally during work roles' (Kahn 1990).

Ultimately, this means that those who are more engaged in their work have a more positive outlook on work, and are more likely to be productive and impact their own and organisational growth and help to create a positive work culture.

Another reason we should look to increase engagement to improve teacher wellbeing is that employees who are more engaged at work have better physical health. There is ample research to suggest that the more engaged we are at work, the more energy we have, the better we function and the less likely we are to experience or complain about work-related health issues such as stress, feeling overworked, or feeling low on energy.

The more engaged we are at work, the more likely we are to attend, meaning we take fewer sick days and are more productive during the time we spend at work.

Knowing that by enhancing work engagement we can positively impact teacher wellbeing, including but not limited to one's physical health, energy levels, job satisfaction and positive workplace culture, we need to seek out ways to ensure we are doing this at an individual and collective level.

At a school level, to increase teacher engagement, teachers need to be involved in the design of the systems, structures and processes they work to and how their time is spent, and know that there is flexibility in the ever-changing circumstances they experience. We often see teacher engagement drop when work becomes too much, too stressful and too overwhelming. This is when we also see negativity creep into school culture. In order to maintain high levels of engagement, we need to ask and listen to what our teachers need, be flexible when things out of our control arise, and continually review and respond to situations that may be causing teachers stress.

Low stress = high engagement
High stress = low engagement

When it comes to engagement, a school or leadership team's main priority should be identifying where stress or friction is occurring, and trying to reduce this as quickly as possible so engagement can rise. The same approach should be taken for individual engagement in our work.

As teachers, if we know that engagement is a combination of our physical, mental and emotional self at work, we have to be prepared to recognise, acknowledge and shift factors that may be contributing to our ability to be engaged. We can't be engaged if we are tired, if we have a negative mindset about an issue or challenge we are experiencing or if we are stressed. This means we need to take responsibility for how engaged we are so we can contribute to our own and others' engagement levels as we work.

To promote self-engagement, it can be useful to look for ways to be creative and try new things, build positive relationships with and collaborate with colleagues, celebrate things that go well, and set goals and find opportunities for growth.

At a school level, to ensure teachers are engaged in their work, seek to give them autonomy and input into what they do, provide time for collaboration between colleagues to occur, seek to know their interests and strengths and find ways to utilise these, and offer opportunities for professional growth and development.

Productivity

When I think of being productive, I think of being time efficient and doing things fast. There is a great sense of achievement in doing things quickly, ticking more things off my list than expected and still having time left over. I pride myself on being able to say 'I have been so productive today'. It gives me a sense of accomplishment and fulfilment that comes from knowing I have done something valuable with my time, and that I am proud of what I achieved (productivity takes care of many areas of my psychological wellbeing – self-acceptance, personal growth and autonomy).

However, I have moments of being productive, and moments of not being able to get into this groove at all. My motivation for different tasks can waver at times, and I can easily find myself procrastinating and being distracted by the most insignificant things.

There are a few statements that are particularly common in the teaching profession:
- 'I don't have enough time.'
- 'There aren't enough hours in the day.'
- 'Teachers are always time poor.'

While many teachers use these statements to describe how they are feeling, to highlight that the workload is too much or to explain why they are tired, there is a hidden message here around productivity. Productivity is our ability to work efficiently in a given timeframe to achieve an output. We want to achieve maximum output with the smallest effort and time.

Let's think about this for a minute: maximum output with the smallest effort. What this really means is, 'How can I do an amazing job, with little effort? How can I plan, mark, assess, collaborate, differentiate and improve student outcomes in the best way possible, within the least amount of time?' What this is suggesting is that we need to be acutely aware of and intentional with the systems, structures and processes we use to complete individual and group tasks. The way in which we do things needs to be efficient (completed in a reasonable amount of time), with ease (not requiring a lot of energy) and effective (has the impact it is designed for). By doing this, not only are we improving productivity, but also our wellbeing.

Being productive requires reflecting on the tasks we do in the time we allocate. To do this we can ask these questions:

- Did I/we do this in the most **efficient** way?
- Did I/we do this **easily**?
- Will this be **effective**?

These are the three Es of productivity: efficient, easy and effective. If each task I complete meets all three of these criteria, I like to think I am being productive; if not, and it's problematic for me, I revaluate my system and/or strategy. When teaching, whether I was planning lessons, making resources, marking books or completing admin tasks, I aimed to be efficient, do it with ease (the path of least resistance) and ensure that the outcome was effective and met its purpose.

If I am honest, this way of operating for me is quite natural. I like systems and structures, and have certain ways of doing things. I am quite ordered in my home, with everything having its place – so much so my siblings often tease me a little and make fun of my need to 'put everything back where it belongs'. Unbeknown to them, though, I don't do this because I am a neat freak; I do this because it allows me to do things with efficiency, ease and effectiveness. I never have to worry where my keys are, where I put my glasses or spend 10 minutes looking for the remote before I can watch television. Everything has a home, and everything follows a system. Now I know this may sound exhausting, but what is important to note is that these systems are designed to save time – and isn't that what every teacher wants? To save time and to have more time? Productivity is not just about getting things done, but about finding ways to save time, while doing things easily, efficiently and effectively.

When things take longer than expected, it can be an opportunity to reflect on efficiency, effectiveness and ease. This may be because of a multitude of things: underestimating the length of the task, procrastination, not having the skills needed, or lack of motivation and engagement. It could be any number of reasons; however, these can also fall into lack of skill or lack of will. Neither of these are good or bad, however, if you find you're not as productive as you would like, it is good to build in a reflective practice on what happened and why. Once you have awareness of what's going on, you can choose to change something, seek help or try a different strategy.

While being productive all the time sounds ideal, we all know that we have moments where we aren't productive. Interestingly, how productive we are can also be connected to our everyday wellbeing.

As we learned when we looked at the WHO's definition of mental health and wellbeing in Chapter 1, productivity is a key contributing factor to optimal wellbeing. Research shows that our state of wellbeing has been linked to higher levels of productivity (Isham, Jackson and Mair 2019). Hence, the more we look after our everyday wellbeing strategies, the more productive we can be.

Productivity, however, should not be confused with busyness. For a long time, this was me. I thought I needed to be busy all the time to do a good job, and was always working. (Remember the introduction where I shared that I just didn't know how to stop? This was busy, not productive.) As Stephen R Covey, author of *The 7 Habits of Highly Effective People*, said, 'It is possible to be busy – very busy – without being very effective.' Busy does not mean productive or effective. We don't want to be busy, we want to be productive. Many teachers have fallen into the trap of being busy all the time, because there is always something to do – but are we always being productive?

The expectation that teachers will be busy isn't helpful for teacher wellbeing. Many teachers and schools hold the belief that if you're not busy, you probably aren't working hard enough. Sound familiar? I know, I have had this thought too. But is it true? These days, I don't think it is. I am not sure how it happened – whether it is because there is always something we *could* do (but not always something we *need* to do), or because it seems more appropriate to be busy than not, or because we have been taught that busy is a normal way to be for a teacher – but continually using the term 'busy' or accepting it as 'normal' is not serving our wellbeing. Wouldn't it be far more beneficial if instead of always being busy, saying we are busy and focusing on the need to be busy, we instead shifted this to being productive?

An interesting thing to note about the word 'busy', and so many other words and phrases we use, is that they often tend to be unhelpful, self-fulling prophecies. If we think we are busy, we will always find ways to be busy. If we think there is always something we need to do, we will make sure we find something to do. If we think we aren't working hard enough, we will work harder. However, what if we instead told ourselves we were productive? Or calm? Or organised? Our language can shape our mental state and even influence what we notice and focus on, and our actions and behaviours – crazy I know, but this is very powerful when it comes to understanding and influencing our own and others' wellbeing. Next time someone asks how you are, instead of responding with 'busy', say 'productive'. Notice what it does for you, and them.

Productivity for teachers is also influenced and impacted by the what, how, why and who of the many systems, structures and processes in a school. As productivity is as much collective responsibility as it is individual responsibility, teams and school leaders need to reflect, review and improve certain ways of doing things when they either inhibit productivity, or if they aren't as effective, efficient or done as easily as can be. This is a practical and relevant way for a school to demonstrate they value teacher wellbeing beyond the subjective, activity-based strategies often utilised, and show that they are prepared to make the changes needed to impact teacher productivity and use of time.

Performance and Growth

To be honest, I was reluctant to include performance in my framework. Performance can have a bit of an icky feel to it. It can bring up ideas and feelings around judgement: 'Am I good enough?', 'Am I doing this right?', 'What will people think?'. Teaching is challenging enough without feeling we are going to be continually judged on our performance.

However, performance is a key part of being a teacher. We have to be open and willing to discuss, share, seek feedback and reflect on the performance of our practice. Performance does not have to be a measure of judgement, or 'Am I good enough?'; in fact, it requires a handful of things we often expect from our students, including a growth mindset and setting goals. One of my favourite questions to ask my students is 'How do you know?'. This is an important question for us to ask as teachers also. How do we know we are doing a great job? It is the reflection on our performance that is key, to support us to identify where we need to grow. As one of my favourite experts in the education space, Dylan Wiliam, says: 'Every teacher needs to improve. Not because they aren't good enough but because they can be even better.' What Wiliam is referring to here is our ability as educators to look at our performance, identify where we can improve, and seek out growth.

This is important also to our psychological wellbeing, with personal growth being one of the six areas of psychological wellbeing in Carol Ryff's scales of psychological wellbeing (we discussed the six areas in Chapter 1). Ryff describes personal growth as feelings of continued development; the sense that one is growing and expanding; openness to new experiences; realisation of one's potential; perceived improvement in self and behaviour over time; and change that reflects greater self-knowledge and effectiveness (Celestine 2021a). My question is, how do we know where we need to improve and grow if we don't look at performance?

Ironically, we measure students' performance all the time. Without judgement or criticism, we find ways for them to show us what they can do; we mark, critique, give them feedback, set goals and targets for them, and test and assess them as required. We also create supportive and engaging environments where students feel safe to make mistakes, try new things, or share and seek out support when they don't know something. In classrooms and schools where this happens well, psychological safety is high. In order to ensure we have teachers who embrace performance and growth in the same way as we expect students to, we need to foster an environment where psychological safety is high.

Amy Edmondson defines psychological safety as 'the belief that one will not be punished or humiliated for speaking up with ideas, questions, concerns, or mistakes and that the team is safe for interpersonal risk-taking' (Edmondson n.d.). Edmondson's research has shown that psychological safety can actually predict both group learning and group performance (Learner Lab n.d.).

Hence, the more safe teachers feel in their ability to share what they would like to do in their classrooms, have the opportunity to enquire and question new ideas or possibilities, share what is worrying them or on their minds and have permission to make errors as they try new things, the better they will perform and grow. With so much emphasis put on student outcomes and data, this is yet again another important reason to invest in better working environments for teachers that build, support and enhance both everyday and workplace wellbeing.

At an individual level, this also means we need to be open-minded and work with a growth mindset as we engage in opportunities to grow and review performance. We have to be willing to reflect, discuss and analyse what and how we teach; we have to be willing to take risks and make changes; and we have to be willing to know that reviewing performance, identifying areas of change and committing to ongoing growth are continual parts of workplace wellbeing.

During this chapter you have discovered why we need to focus on teacher wellbeing. Whether it is your own wellbeing or the wellbeing of teachers in your school, it is evident that the reason to prioritise this is more than a one-word answer. While we all want to be happy, fit for purpose teacher wellbeing matters because it impacts our ability to be engaged in what we do, be productive with our time and perform to a high standard – and when we do these things well, this impacts our overall wellbeing.

The connection between these three things and workplace wellbeing is similar to a spider trapping a fly in its web:, the more we loop around and around, the stronger it will become (see figure 5).

Figure 5: The Engagement, Productivity and Performance for Workplace Wellbeing Cycle

Chapter Summary

- The purpose of teacher wellbeing is to support everyday and workplace wellbeing.
- Everyday wellbeing encompasses energy and function, resilience and emotional regulation.
- Workplace wellbeing is about being 'fit for purpose' and focuses on engagement, productivity and performance and growth.
- Engagement can improve health, reduce stress and boost productivity.
- Productivity is our ability to complete tasks in a given time frame with efficiency, effectiveness, and ease.
- Performance and growth requires a growth mindset, and high psychological safety.

From Theory to Action

1. Using the statements below, give yourself a score out of 10 (1 being low, 10 being high).
2. Looking at the lower numbers first, ask yourself, what number out of 10 would you like to be at? For example, if you are a 2/10 in a certain area, you may aim for a 5/10.
3. Ask yourself, 'What could I do to achieve my target number?' You may like to write this down or use this to set some areas of growth or goals for yourself.

Engagement:
- I enjoy working at my school.
- I regularly contribute to my team.
- I feel supported by others.
- I work collaboratively with others.
- I feel like I am growing as a professional at this school.
- When I feel low engagement, I know how to shift my state.

Productivity:
- I accomplish tasks (for example, planning, marking and reports) in a timely manner.
- I deliver high-quality work by the required time.
- I work efficiently with the time I am given.
- I can prioritise tasks and workload.
- I actively seek out new ways to do things to enhance productivity and save time.
- When I am not as productive as I would like, I reflect on this and change something, ask for help or try a new strategy.

Performance and growth:
- I set regular goals and seek feedback and support to meet these.
- I am open to and regularly seek out professional development to learn new ways of doing things and implement these in my classroom.
- I regularly use student growth data (both formative and summative) to reflect on my practice as a teacher.
- I regularly engage with the AITSL standards as a way to reflect on and improve my teaching practice.
- I ask my students, colleagues and school leaders for feedback on my teaching.
- If I don't teach as well as I would like, I am able to reflect on this and try something new or ask for help.

These questions are a guide to help you reflect on your own engagement, productivity and performance. It is common for your scores to fluctuate over time. However, if you find your scores are consistently low in one or more areas, this may highlight something you wish to focus on.

Chapter 3

Where We Got it Wrong

> *If someone is going down the wrong road,*
> *he doesn't need motivation to speed him up.*
> *What he needs is education to turn him around.*
> – Jim Rohn

In this chapter, we're going to look at 10 mistakes we have made when it comes to addressing teacher wellbeing. I acknowledge that what I have to say may include some bold statements, but I think it is important. As with any change management process, we must recognise where we have gone wrong so we can begin to look at things differently. This is not about finger-pointing or blame, but an opportunity to recognise and acknowledge what has occurred so far. I have no doubt that some of these 'mistakes' might push your thinking a little, and to be honest, that is the point. We have to be able to have real, brave, vulnerable conversations about teacher wellbeing if we really want it to change. So here we go …

Mistake #1

We collected a lot of data, but did nothing with it

Teacher wellbeing isn't a new thing, although post-Covid it has certainly become more prevalent. As teaching has become more demanding, we have seen statistics like '50% of teachers leave in their first five years' being reported online and in the media. What is interesting, though, is that despite this now being a well-known statistic, nothing has really changed. Teachers are still leaving the profession. In 2017, the ABC reported 53% of teachers who hold a degree weren't teaching and 20% of new graduates never began their teaching career (Stroud 2017). In another article the ABC reported that in 2021, 1100 teaching positions in New South Wales alone were never filled (Wilson and Carabetta 2022). Those statistics, five years apart, both with alarming numbers and both mentioning a teacher shortage, are worth paying attention to.

Over time, increasing pressures have undoubtedly impacted teacher wellbeing. Despite schools and teachers doing the absolute best they can, we still have a profession whose members, for the most part, feel tired, overwhelmed and underappreciated.

A few years back I was doing some research in this space as part of an emerging leaders' program. In among all the papers I read, I discovered there was very little research exploring why 50% of teachers were leaving, and where they were going. One thing that I did come across, though, was that many teachers were leaving because they felt unsupported. In a survey of over 2500 teachers published by Monash University in 2019, the three main reasons for teachers leaving the profession were said to be workload; health and wellbeing; and feeling underappreciated and the poor status of the profession.

Even though health and wellbeing feature as separate pieces of data in this report, I would argue that workload and feeling underappreciated also negatively impact the health and wellbeing of teachers. When this occurs time and time again, and multiple things start to impact our health and wellbeing, we are never far from burnout.

So many of us know and have experienced the burnout, overwhelm and stress that comes with teaching, and it doesn't take much to find evidence of this. According to the Australian Institute for Teaching and School Leadership (AITSL; 2022), in a 2021 survey completed by 571 educators from across Australia and from multiple systems, 80% of educators said their work/life balance was either 'less than ideal' or 'non-existent; job satisfaction levels for educators had dropped from 91% in 2017 to 63% in 2021; and just under half (48%) reported they 'think about leaving' fairly often or most of the time over the course of a year.

The stats are in, so what are we going to do about it?

Mistake #2

We waited for the system to rescue us

If the statistics tell us anything, it's that the system, unfortunately, hasn't responded to the data. Data is useless unless we use and respond to it. Unfortunately, reporting it in research papers and newspaper headlines is not putting it to good use – we need to respond to it within schools in order for it to have impact.

While the system itself has a lot to answer for, unfortunately, it's not an easy fix. Along with the above, things such as pay, working conditions and public perception also contribute to teacher wellbeing. However, what we need here goes far beyond what we can achieve by wishing, waiting or hoping for the system to change. To be honest, we just don't have time for that. If we are on the verge of a teacher shortage crisis, it is too late to wait for the system to do something. We, you, me, teachers and leaders, have to do something.

What can be done right now is the change we can make at an individual and school level regarding our own wellbeing and the wellbeing of our staff. We can make changes to our everyday wellbeing that allow us to feel more energised, less stressed and more fulfilled. We can make changes that improve workplace wellbeing and allow us to work more productively, have more time, feel more engaged and grow as professionals. Schools can also make changes to the systems, structures and processes that exist around how things are done.

If we all band together to work on improving our own wellbeing, when we come together to work, teach and support each other the effect can be pretty big. The same can be said for school wellbeing. Each school plays a key role in supporting the wellbeing of all staff, as well as students. When a school makes a commitment to improving whole-school wellbeing, there is a direct link between this and an improvement in teaching and learning, student engagement and staff working collaboratively.

So many of us look to and spend time and energy focusing on the system itself that we overlook the most important and perhaps easiest thing to change: ourselves, and our schools. It is our wellbeing that must become a priority – that of the teacher. If we can make a change with teacher wellbeing, I think we can dramatically change the way we experience each day, week and perhaps our whole careers as educators.

Note: this does not excuse or suggest we should not work on changes at a system level. In fact, we must keep doing this as well. We need to continue fighting for what we deserve and what is right, while at the same time making changes where we can.

Mistake #3

We waited until we hit rock bottom

Improving our mental health and wellbeing was never intended to occur only when something was wrong. Martin Seligman's work in the field of positive psychology has been paramount to creating the shift we are now seeing regarding self-development, ongoing personal improvement and, as he calls it, 'flourishing'. Prior to World War II, according to Seligman, Parks and Steen (2004), American psychology had three objectives: to cure mental illness, to make relatively untroubled people happier and to study genius and high talent. However, following World War II, psychology shifted to primarily focus on mental illness and those who were suffering. Because of this, focusing on people's wellbeing and making them happier was left to the side.

This has caused many of us to believe that we only need to improve our wellbeing if there is something wrong, if we are unhappy or if we feel we are suffering, when in fact, this was never the intention behind the initial work of psychology. This is why we feel we have to push on or wait until we are at breaking point, or tell ourselves 'things aren't that bad'. We shouldn't have to get to breaking point to feel we are worthy of asking for help, to admit there is too much on our plate or that we need a break. Nor should we expect this of others. We need to normalise the fact that wanting to improve because we have a right to flourish and feel good is enough. We shouldn't think that we or others need to fall apart or have mental health issues before we offer or accept help. It is okay to ask for help, it is okay to not be able to do it all and it is okay to want more, even when things seem pretty good already.

This shift we now see towards positive psychology can very much be credited to Martin Seligman as president of the American Psychology Association beginning in 1996. When Seligman undertook this position, he made it his mission to focus on the idea that everyone has a right to flourish, and that we need to enhance both individual and community wellbeing: 'The ultimate goal of positive psychology is to make people happier by understanding and building positive emotion, gratification and meaning' (Seligman, Parks and Steen 2004).

This is significantly different to most of the work we have been focusing on in schools regarding wellbeing, and as already mentioned it goes far beyond the one-off wellbeing 'events' we so often see. This too highlights that the work required to improve our wellbeing cannot be done by someone else, it must be done by us. Yes, there are things school leaders can do to ensure the structures and systems within the organisation support us to work on our wellbeing, but ultimately it is up to us. Our wellbeing should not be an afterthought, a reaction or something we will work on tomorrow; it must become part of who we are and how we operate if we want to see long-term, sustainable change both for ourselves and within our schools.

Mistake #4

We confused self-care and wellbeing

For too long, self-care has been the focus, the strategy and the solution for a teacher or staff group with low wellbeing. It is the approach many schools take as they implement things like morning teas, birthday lunches, Friday drinks or meeting-free weeks, and then encourage staff to get a massage, go for a walk or take the afternoon off to read a book. While these things are nice, and make us feel good in the moment, they are not going to help any teacher realise their ability, cope with daily stress, be more productive or contribute to the community.

We have to understand that for many of us, our understanding of wellbeing has actually been self-care. Please know you are not to blame if you have confused wellbeing and self-care in the past. If anything, I would say that social media has contributed significantly to a lack of understanding as it has provided multiple examples of misinformation that people too easily latch on to. It is the quotes we all love and have printed on our walls, the 'Teacher Wellbeing Checklists' we can easily print off and hand out to our teacher buddies as something to do together 'because this year will be different', or the gift packs leaders whip up and hope that the 'tea bag to help you relax' and 'chocolate to make you feel better' keeps your wellbeing intact for the next few weeks. Please know I too have been this teacher and leader, with my checklists and chocolates to hand out. It is this, and more, with all the cute graphics and pretty gift bags, that has led us to believe that this is what wellbeing is, when in fact, it is so much more.

In breaking down our understanding of wellbeing and being open to realising that there is a distinct difference between wellbeing and self-care – that wellbeing is not a fancy version of self-care, nor it is just what we do – we can be more targeted and intentional with our strategies. Wellbeing is who we are and how we feel. It is improved by the unique, long-term, sustainable strategies we use to continually improve our wellbeing.

Optimal wellbeing cannot be achieved by having a 'Wellbeing Wall' in the staffroom, getting everyone to put on activewear and practise their downward dog or ensuring there is always chocolate in the staffroom to 'get us to 3 pm'. It is much bigger, deeper and far more complex than this.

Mistake #5

We underestimated the work of wellbeing

I have no doubt that some of you reading this book have tried various things to improve your wellbeing. You may feel like your wellbeing is quite optimal (which is great!); you may even work in a school that has a wellbeing strategy; or perhaps your school has Friday morning teas and the odd meeting-free week designed to take care of how you feel and 'fix' the wellbeing issues you face.

For our wellbeing to be paramount, though, we must actively decide to work on our wellbeing. We must decide how we want to feel and how we want to be, and bit by bit begin to make changes that will enhance our wellbeing each and every day. We also need to acknowledge that this takes time, requires patience, and may involve some trial and error to figure out what does and doesn't work. We must also honour and accept where we are; be willing to stick it out even if it isn't as easy, pretty or fun as we have been led to believe; and be ready to do the work needed.

The truth is, wellbeing can be complicated, abstract and hard to define. It also looks vastly different to everyone and cannot be solved with a one-size-fits-all approach. We all have different needs, different priorities in our life and different things that impact our wellbeing, which is why we can't all be prescribed the same wellbeing checklist. It just doesn't work like that, and we have to stop thinking it is that simple. Not everyone likes yoga, wants to meditate, or has the time to exercise each day, and that is okay. Wellbeing is far more diverse than this.

Further to this, the work of wellbeing at a school level does not solely lie in the staff meetings we dedicate to this topic, but also in our daily operational organisation. Our wellbeing is reflected in how we do the work of teaching. This is why the long-term change we need is challenging. It requires work in response to our daily operations: how we organise our day, how we ask teachers to plan, how our teams function, the support teachers receive. All of these things and more, which we have seen as teaching and learning factors, are very much things that impact wellbeing, and that need to be considered when we commit to engaging in the work of wellbeing.

Mistake #6

It became us and them, when in fact it is us – all of us

I have, more than once, heard comments from teachers that highlight a perception that school leaders don't care about teacher wellbeing. I have heard more than one teacher say, 'My leaders/principal don't care about my wellbeing.' Before we look at wellbeing as a whole-school approach, it is important to note that this statement is not true.

I can assure you, no school leader is sitting in their office asking themselves, 'How can I negatively impact the wellbeing of my staff?' Wellbeing – especially as defined by and understood through the lenses of subjective and psychological wellbeing, and everyday and workplace wellbeing – will be new for many. All any school leader or teacher has been doing is the absolute best they can with the perhaps limited knowledge and resources they have. We must remember that school leaders, first and foremost, are teachers too. They aren't trained in HR or business management, and most aren't experts in psychology and wellbeing – they are maths teachers, English teachers, science teachers or primary school teachers who have taken on the role of leading a school.

I think we also need to acknowledge that school leaders face a considerable amount of pressure that we as teachers may not realise, and that there are things we don't know (and don't need to know). There are multiple pressures that come with leading a school, and teacher wellbeing, as important as it is, is only one piece of a very large, demanding list.

To move forward from thinking school leaders don't care, we need to do a few things. Firstly, we need to unite as educators, and acknowledge that everyone is doing the best they can with the information, knowledge resources and time that they have. Secondly, we need to practise compassion, for ourselves and each other. The work of wellbeing is challenging and we need to support each other. Thirdly, we need to talk to each other, and listen to each other. We need to put aside time for conversations about wellbeing, how we feel and how we work, and we need time together to figure out what we need to do next.

Once we understand that wellbeing is a balance of both subjective and psychological wellbeing, our everyday and workplace wellbeing, and unite, act with compassion and make time to listen and talk to each other, we can begin to work on how we can change both individually and collectively as a school.

Mistake #7

We tried to outsource our wellbeing when we needed to take responsibility

The responsibility of wellbeing has been passed from system, to principal, to leader, to teacher and back again. While everyone plays a role, outsourcing your wellbeing to someone else is not a smart idea. Do you really want someone you don't know making decisions about how you feel, think or behave? No, I didn't think so – so you can't continue to hand over your wellbeing to others.

I know this may be hard to hear, but your everyday wellbeing is your responsibility. Yep, yours. Not your teaching partner's, team leader's or principal's responsibility. Your wellbeing is your responsibility, and someone else's wellbeing is their responsibility. Now, of course, other things may impact our wellbeing and how we feel, but we get to decide the actions we take, what we focus on, the meaning we attach to things, the conversations we have and how we spend our time. We get to decide a lot of what makes up our wellbeing, and it is our individual responsibility to make sure we are doing the best we can to look after all areas of our wellbeing. This means you must learn about your own wellbeing, be open to making changes, and do the work that needs to be done – even when it is hard (because at times it will be). This also means that even though you may suspect someone needs to work on their wellbeing, you can't do it for them. You can't do the work for someone else and someone else can't do the work for you.

Does this mean it's everyone on their own, then? Absolutely not. As I explained earlier, it is essential we work together, support each other and look out for each other. That being said, we must also acknowledge that the state of our own wellbeing will impact others. If we are in a negative frame of mind, not working collaboratively or cohesively, not being kind or not contributing to the team, we will impact how others feel. The same is true if we are kinder, more open, working collaboratively, contributing to and building positive relationships: our state of wellbeing impacts those around us. This does not mean we need to be 'happy' all the time, but if we are experiencing a more challenging time, we need to be mindful of how that may cause us to interact with others, and take responsibility for our actions in this space.

It is also important to add that even though we are responsible for our own wellbeing, collectively we are also responsible for school wellbeing.

Mistake #8

We underestimated the systems, structures and processes we use

The systems, structures and processes we use impact our wellbeing, especially workplace wellbeing. As individuals, teams and whole schools the way we do things matters. How we plan, collaborate, design and resource lessons, organise timetables, collect and enter data, mark books ... everything we do is a result of a system, structure or process that supports our workplace wellbeing (or doesn't). We need to pay more attention to these factors; develop skills to reflect on, audit and make changes; and be willing to do things differently.

While leaders can't *do* wellbeing for someone else, they can make sure that they have created the systems, structures and processes needed to support teachers. This means encouraging, allowing and expecting others to work on their everyday and workplace wellbeing and putting things in place to allow this to happen. However, just because the systems, structures and processes are there doesn't mean all people will access or use all these things. People will do what they are ready for, when they are ready for it, even if we would prefer they did something different. As a leader, our job is to make sure that when they are ready, everything is in place to support them; until that moment comes, we simply hold space for them to be and occasionally remind them that when they are ready, we are here for them.

In a more practical sense, we must regularly review and reflect on how we get things done. Are we being efficient, effective and doing things with ease? Or are the ways we are doing things causing us or others stress? Are people confused or unclear? Is there a double (or triple) up of things being done, or are tasks taking too long to complete? We need to ask these questions regularly and often about things that happen in our school, so we can continually look for more effective, efficient and easier ways of doing things. The more this happens, the more productive we feel, the better our wellbeing.

Mistake #9

We tried to put everyone in the same box

It is important we respect and understand everyone's unique wellbeing journey and that people will be at different places, choose to focus on different things and want to achieve different results. This is why wellbeing is not a one-size-fits-all approach: we can't give everyone the same checklist to complete, continue with ad-hoc activities or keep focusing on subjective wellbeing. It's both subjective and psychological wellbeing and everyday and workplace wellbeing, all at once, and it's different for everyone.

When we begin to think about wellbeing as not just what we do to make sure we are happy all the time, or to pick us up when we feel down, but something that is linked to fulfilment, purpose, connection and growth, it opens up a whole new way to approach the work we need to do both as teachers, and in schools as a collective. It allows us to not only focus on what we do, but also who we are, who we want to be, how we feel and how we want to feel. With this, we open a whole new way of thinking about, planning for and working towards improving our wellbeing. Gone is the idea that we should just tick a few things off a list to make us feel better; instead, we realise that this work is happening all the time. It exists in our thinking, our conversations, the people we connect with, how we spend our time, what we belong to, what we focus on, our decisions, our actions and the deliberate, intentional daily changes and decisions we make.

If we all agree that there are two sides to wellbeing, the subjective and psychological, and that chasing after feeling happy isn't really working, then we can begin to see the bigger picture and work together on real change – change that is long-term, sustainable and will influence the system. We can realise that while it is important to keep doing things that make us feel good, so too it is important to work on our fulfilment, meaning, connection and continual growth. By doing this, what we now have is the opportunity to change how we view and create wellbeing in the space of education: for our teachers, for our leaders, for our students and for our wider school community. This is where the real work of long-term, sustainable change for our wellbeing can begin.

Mistake #10

We adopted too many frameworks, approaches and models and forgot who we were

Along with the term 'flourishing', Seligman is also well known for his PERMA model. It describes the building blocks to improving wellbeing and achieving happiness: positive emotions, engagement, relationships, meaning and achievement. This is just one of the many frameworks that now exists to work on your wellbeing.

After looking at a significant number of models and frameworks, I've seen that there are eight main areas of wellbeing. Not all appear in every framework (as already noted, Seligman has five in his PERMA model), and not all are called the same thing, with some words being used interchangeably. The eight most-used areas are: physical, emotional, financial, environmental, social, spiritual, career and intellectual. Other common terms include relational, vocational and mental wellbeing. Again, this is why wellbeing is complicated and can't be a one-size-fits-all approach.

I have seen many schools use wellbeing frameworks – for whole-school, staff and students – for the wrong reasons: they look good, the school down the road uses it, someone chose it (but didn't consult staff), it was well resourced, they needed a quick fix or it landed in their inbox at the right time. These are not good reasons for adopting a framework or approach.

To be honest, I don't think it really matters if you have a framework, approach or use an acronym. What matters is the following:

1. Your framework or approach should be school-wide – something that applies to students, teachers and other staff. We don't need different frameworks or approaches for each.
2. Whatever you use should be aligned to your school values and a reflection of the culture you foster. Wellbeing is who you are, not just what you do, and this needs to be reflected in your wellbeing approach or framework.
3. It should allow everyone to access it in a way that meets their individual needs; wellbeing is not a one-size-fits-all approach.
4. It must be explicitly taught, understood and actioned by everyone, including staff, students and the wider school community. Having it on a poster or website is not enough.
5. It must be measurable and impactful. If it isn't working, change it.
6. It should be a part of what you do every day, not an add-on or an underused component. We also don't need numerous additional programs; we just need to better use what we have.
7. It must be evident in all aspects of school life, including teaching and learning, behaviour management, policies, strategic plans and priorities, staff and student goals and decision-making processes.
8. It is a collective approach, meaning it must be developed, reflected and/or improved upon by all stakeholders including staff, students and the wider school community.
9. It needs to be visible and evident in the language, actions and decision-making of all.

Ultimately, it is not the *what* of teacher wellbeing we need to focus on, but the *how, why* and *who*.

Now we have established the most significant mistakes we have made, we can begin our journey of learning and understanding more about teacher wellbeing, what it really is and what we can do about it.

Chapter Summary

- We have made some mistakes; let's acknowledge and learn from these.
- Pointing the finger, blaming, justifying or denying these mistakes will not help us move forward.
- Everyone has been doing the best they can with the resources they have.
- Change in all areas requires individual and collective responsibility.
- We have to have brave, real, vulnerable conversations to help us change and move forward.

From Theory to Action

Ten mistakes, 10 things to reflect on, 10 ways to begin to make change.

This task is simple: go back and read each mistake again, note down your biggest take-away and one thing you could, or would, like to change or implement right now. It could be something practical, an idea you would like to explore, or a mindset shift you would like to make.

10 Wellbeing Mistakes to Reflect On

Mistake	Biggest Take-Away	One Thing to Change or Implement
Mistake #1 We collected a lot of data, but did nothing with it		
Mistake #2 We waited for the system to rescue us		

Mistake #3 We waited until we hit rock bottom		
Mistake #4 We confused self-care and wellbeing		
Mistake #5 We underestimated the work of wellbeing		
Mistake #6 It became us and them, when in fact it is us – all of us		
Mistake #7 We tried to outsource our wellbeing when we needed to take responsibility		
Mistake #8 We underestimated the systems, structures and processes we use		
Mistake #9 We tried to put everyone in the same box		
Mistake #10 We adopted too many frameworks, approaches and models and forgot who we were		

Part 2

The Work of Wellbeing

The work of wellbeing is something we need to give time to. We are trying to find what works for us and what allows us to feel like we have our wellbeing in an optimal state most of the time – and how to return to that optimal state when things pull us down.

Having already explored various definitions of wellbeing in Part 1 and taken the time to reflect on and build our own definition, we can now begin to look at the practical strategies, daily habits and non-negotiables we can implement to keep our wellbeing at an optimal state.

Before we dive into the practical elements, though, I want to take the idea of a wellbeing definition one step further. Having spent many years trying to hack my own wellbeing strategy and figure out what works for me and what doesn't, I often find I am in my most optimal wellbeing state when I am feeling calm, content and grounded in myself. In the workspace, my wellbeing is optimal when I feel fulfilled, motivated, engaged and productive.

Your optimal state of wellbeing should allow you to function easily and manage normal stress through adaptive resilience strategies, and give you the awareness needed to regulate your emotions. By working on these three things, you are continually balancing your state of wellbeing until it resides at its point of equilibrium.

Your wellbeing point of equilibrium is your set point, where you like to be most often, the place that feels like home. This is ultimately what we are chasing when we are working on our wellbeing.

As figure 6 demonstrates, life is full of experiences that pull us above or below our set point, our point of equilibrium. Through the work of wellbeing, our strategies, we are able to stabilise and come back to our point of equilibrium. Each of us need to be able to identify and actively take action through subjective and psychological approaches that support our ability to reach our point of equilibrium. The more we do this, the easier it becomes, and the quicker we are able to come back home.

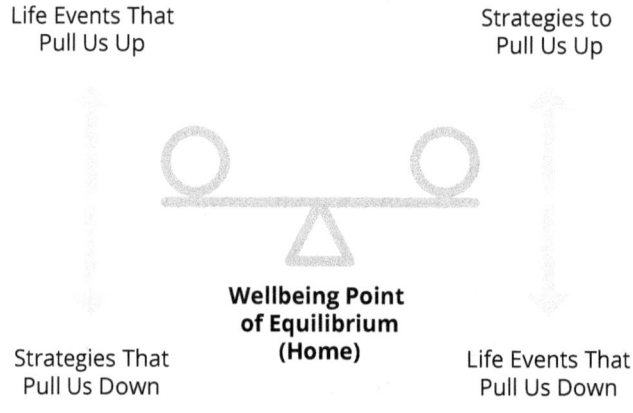

Figure 6: Wellbeing Point of Equilibrium

The work of wellbeing comprises of both everyday and workplace wellbeing. Having already looked at workplace wellbeing in Part 1, and developed our understanding of engagement, productivity, and performance and growth, Part 2 of this book will focus on the three main areas of everyday wellbeing:
- energy and function
- resilience
- emotional regulation.

As you learn more about these three areas of everyday wellbeing, I want you to understand why, out of all the components of wellbeing that exist, these three matter the most.

Firstly, they are all related and intertwined. Each of these areas supports the others. Your energy levels impact your ability to choose adaptive resilience strategies, your resilience strategies impact your emotions, and your emotions impact everything. The connection between each is strong and each is equally important.

Secondly, imagine these three areas of everyday wellbeing as supporting your mind, body and soul. Wellbeing, at its most simple level, is ensuring we have these three areas flourishing. When we do this, we are taking care of who we are on a physical, mental and emotional level. These are the foundational areas to our everyday wellbeing.

Thirdly, all other areas of wellbeing you hear of – for example, financial, occupational, environmental and so on – can be attended to, or may happen naturally, when these three areas are in optimal state.

Table 4 explains how mind, body and soul support the areas of everyday wellbeing: energy and function, resilience and emotional regulation.

Holistic Approach	Areas of Health	Wellbeing Focus
Mind – our cognitive self, our thoughts, which create our reality and perception of life.	Mental health – how we make decisions and think clearly.	Resilience – our ability to choose supportive strategies when faced with challenges or obstacles.
Body – a complex system designed to support our heart and brain to be alive.	Physical health – how well our body functions.	Energy and function – our ability to complete daily tasks without feeling depleted and to reduce illness.
Soul – who we are in our true essence, removing ego and human conditioning.	Emotional health – how we manage emotions.	Emotional regulation – our ability to recognise, understand, process and regulate emotions when needed.

Table 4: Mind, Body, Soul and Everyday Wellbeing

Ultimately, through our everyday wellbeing strategies, we are trying to take care of our mind, body, and soul, the essence of who we are. With wellbeing as we know it being complicated, coming back to these three areas provides a succinct yet powerful framework for us to be able to thrive.

As we work through each of these areas in the following chapters, you will discover the art and science behind the work of wellbeing. While these areas come with a significant amount of science to back them up and research proving why it is necessary to work on each, it is the art of balancing them and putting theory into action that makes the science impactful.

You have to do the work of wellbeing for it to make a difference. You have to know your non-negotiables and what works for you; you have to commit to building daily habits that, over time, become part of who you are; and you have to be ready to experiment to find what works for you.

In some ways, wellbeing is an experiment – there is no right or wrong way, as long as the work you do is helping you to come back to your point of equilibrium; to come back home to where you feel most aligned with who you are, mind, body and soul.

Chapter 4

Energy and Function

Everything you do to improve your physical wellbeing will have a positive impact on how good you feel about yourself.
– Brian Tracy

As I shared in the introduction, I have been through periods of extremely low energy as a teacher. From not being able to fall asleep at night, even though earlier that afternoon I had to lie on my kitchen floor for 30 minutes after walking through the front door, to experiencing brain fog and finding simple tasks such as getting out of the car exhausting. However, I also know what it is like to experience optimal energy, to feel ready to face the day and look forward to it, and to have enough energy to keep up with my own interests beyond the school day.

Mastering my own energy levels, knowing how my energy feels in my body and understanding the things that give me energy or drain me of energy has taken me a few years to learn. It has taken a combination of allowing myself to rest when needed, learning to say no to things that aren't right for me, and trial and error.

Many educators fall victim to the idea that we just have to keep going. It is normal to hear phrases such as, 'Just make it to Friday' or, 'Not long until holidays now'. I once had a colleague who would greet us with a countdown to holidays every Monday. My 'Good morning, happy Monday' greeting would be followed by 'Only six weeks to go' (or however many weeks it was until the next holidays rolled around). I understand why we do this, but I also struggle to comprehend why we are always counting down until we can get away from a job so many of us love. I know there is a lightness in this, or maybe even a little hope each of us hang on to, but I do wonder: if we are always counting down until we can finally stop, rest and recover, how does this impact our energy levels?

It's very rare for me to count down until Friday or the holidays these days. Don't get me wrong: on Thursday it's worthy to note that tomorrow is Friday, and on Week 9 it's appropriate to mention that next week is the last week – we are human and have to keep it real, plus everyone loves the chance to switch off, sleep in and have spare time during the day. What I am mindful of, though, if I catch myself thinking about how many days or weeks are left, is whether I am counting down to get away from work, or counting down because I have something that I am really looking forward to. These two mindset approaches are very different, as each impacts how we feel and how much energy we have.

If we are only ever counting down to the weekend or holidays because we see those as our only time to rest, recharge, get away from work and feel like we can be ourselves, we are not looking after our energy during the week. If, however, we are counting down because we have something exciting planned, that will impact us differently.

When I catch myself counting down because I am exhausted or feel like I can't go on, I know this is a sign I haven't been doing all the things I need to do to look after my energy – and that while a restful weekend may be in order, so may be some reflection on what I have been doing to maintain my energy to the level at which I function best. Sometimes, this may be something I can identify easily – for example, I was away the weekend before, I haven't been sleeping well, it is report-writing week and I have a little more on my plate, or maybe I have something going on in my personal life that is impacting how I feel. At times, I might not be able to figure out why. Perhaps it is just a matter of slowing down a little and coming back to what I know to be the foundations of my physical wellness, how I maintain these and what I need to do to function optimally each day.

Foundations for Optimal Energy Framework

Many wellbeing and wellness frameworks reference physical health, physical body or something similar as a key component to looking after your wellbeing.

Looking after your physical health and body – including having a good sleep routine, staying hydrated, intentionally moving your body each day, making time to rest and choosing nutritious foods – impacts your overall wellbeing. Not only do these things work in a preventative way for our physical health, they also improve our mental and emotional health as well. Being physically healthy and moving our body can help to reduce stress and overwhelm, increase energy levels, support us to think more clearly, and increase productivity. Research has also shown that people report higher health-related quality of life scores when engaging in physical activity (Bize, Johnson and Plotnikoff 2007).

When we are looking at our own energy levels and how we function each day both in and out of the classroom, it is essential to know what we require and what this looks like to us as individuals. While I love running, yoga, and meditation, and know the benefits from these activities significantly impact my wellbeing, they do not work for everyone. You have to find what works for you.

Now, this may not seem like rocket science, but the essential elements we need to feel energised and to function our best are perhaps the most challenging to master and maintain on a daily basis. Each of the five areas in the Foundations for Optimal Energy Framework (figure 7 overleaf) – nutrition, movement, hydration, sleep and rest – are like pieces of a puzzle: they all go together to ensure you have the energy you need. They are the foundations to how you feel, think and be.

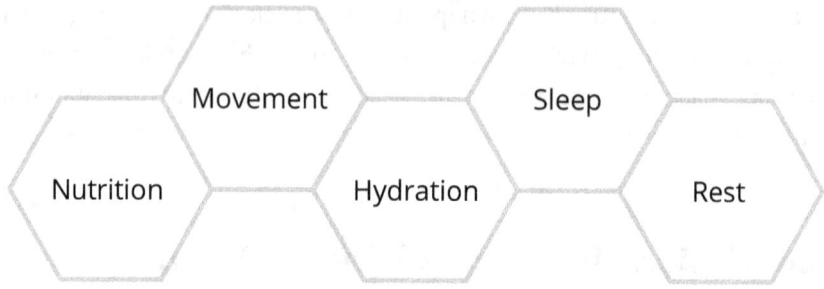

Figure 7: Foundations for Optimal Energy Framework

Let's look at each of the components in turn.

Nutrition

The foods we eat impact both our mind and body, which means we need to make intentional choices throughout the day. Food is fuel; and as we are often *go, go, go* and on supercharge for just about every minute of the day, we have to make sure we are getting the right fuel. If we don't eat the right foods for both mind and body, we can experience repercussions in many ways.

We have all found ourselves with brain fog in the middle of a planning meeting, or succumbed to the 3 pm slump, and relied on sugary foods to get us through the afternoon – leaving us hangry as we arrive home after work. We all know too well that feeling of running straight to the pantry to try to eat ourselves happy, or finding ourselves snapping and on edge until we finally make time to eat – neither of which are the best possible scenario. Nutritious food is essential for feeling, thinking and functioning well. It is easy to understand that we need fuel to move, however the food we eat also impacts our brain, not just our body. Our brain is actually just as important when it comes to food choices as it uses more energy than other organs and accounts for 20% of our total energy expenditure (Swaminathan 2008). Hence the term 'brain foods' – yes, they are a real thing.

According to Queensland Health (2019):

> *Following a healthy pattern of eating is linked with better stress management, improved sleep quality, increased concentration, and better mental wellbeing in general. Just as our food choices affect our physical and mental wellbeing, the opposite is also true – we're more likely to follow a healthy diet when we're in a good headspace.*

I am not a dietician or nutritionist, so will not prescribe a diet or certain foods; however, I do think we all know what foods we should eat most of, and what foods we should reduce or avoid during the work day. While I don't believe in eliminating any foods or food groups (unless for medical, cultural or ethical reasons), I do try to stick to eating a variety of fruits and vegetables each day, and whole foods where possible. I also reduce my intake of saturated fats and high-processed and sugary foods: I save these for after dinner or on weekends. These are not brain foods and do not help our mind or body to function at their best.

Movement

Moving our body each day has a significant impact on our overall health. Be it strenuous exercise or a gentle walk, movement nurtures our mind, body and soul. While keeping us physically fit, movement can also help to reduce stress and anxiety, improve brain function, reduce the risk of dementia, improve our state of mind, boost our immune system, and help us sleep better; this list is endless. There are also additional benefits to moving outdoors as well as exercising with other people. Further to this, research has suggested that physical exercise may reduce burnout and exhaustion.

The way you choose to move your body is again not a one-size-fit-all approach. Movement to improve wellbeing does not mean we all have to do yoga or take up running – the two most common things people tell me they think they 'should' be doing to look after their physical health. Yoga and running are not for everyone, and they are not the only ways you can move. What's important is that you find what works for you, what you enjoy, what makes you feel good, and what benefits your physical, mental and emotional health in one. This could be running and yoga, or it could be hiking, cycling, walking, playing ultimate frisbee or surfing. It doesn't matter what it is, as long as you move your body each day, enjoy what you do and are feeling the benefits.

Hydration

'Eight glasses of water a day – does that include coffee?'

The ultimate aim here is to stay hydrated, not drink water. Being hydrated is the cure to many common issues that get in the way of optimal energy and function, resulting in feeling tired or fatigued, having sugar cravings or experiencing brain fog. Now before you head out and buy a new water bottle (that can help though), there are a few tips and tricks you can implement in your day to help you stay hydrated while avoiding the need to rush to the toilet every hour (and yes, I know this is a real teacher issue, and why some teachers don't drink enough water or stay hydrated – and no, this is not okay).

As well as guzzling water each day, there are other things that can help you stay hydrated. Foods high in water content are a great addition to your daily meals to keep hydration up – things like watermelon, oranges, cucumber, tomatoes and celery are great. If you're not a fan of water, drinks such as diet sodas and juice are okay, although they are possibly not the best in nutritional value; tea or coffee will do the trick too (Soong 2022).

Again, it is about finding what works for you, and paying attention to how your body feels. If you're not sure if you are hydrated enough, the pee test is always worth considering: if you're urinating every two to four hours, the output is light-coloured and there's significant volume, then you're probably well hydrated (Soong 2022).

Sleep

Possibly the most crucial of all, sleep has a significant impact on all areas of our health. Not getting enough sleep can have an alarming impact on our body's ability to function well, with things such as alcohol, coffee, electronics and stress impacting our ability to fall asleep. These things also impact our ability to enter rapid eye movement (REM) sleep, which is needed to feel well rested.

REM sleep is the time in which dreams occur and when our brain processes information from the day. Not engaging in REM sleep can negatively impact our memory, mental state and mood (National Sleep Foundation 2020).

If we don't have enough sleep, we also increase cortisol in our body, which impacts our sympathetic nervous system, causing us to be in fight, flight or freeze mode. When this happens, we are less likely to manage everyday stress, be productive or think clearly. Overall, we should aim for somewhere between seven and nine hours' sleep a night. I know this may be problematic for some teachers, with sleep being a consistent and ongoing issue in our profession due to the continuous demands, stress and pressures we face keeping us up at night, but it needs to be a priority. If sleep is an issue for you, there are few different strategies I suggest you try to help you get the sleep you need:

- *Develop a sleep routine.* Just as when we were younger and had a sleep routine – something like 'dinner, bath, story, bed', as my mum used to say – we need to do the same as adults. Too many of us try to go from wide awake to asleep in a matter of minutes without giving ourselves time to wind down.
- *Turn off the lights.* Our bodies are designed to work with the sun, yet nowadays with electricity and the ability to have light as required, our brain and body don't receive the natural trigger signs of it being evening as they would if we were all still living in caves. To help send the signals to your mind and body that it is nearly time to sleep, dim the lights or use lamps at least 30 to 60 minutes before bed.
- *Reduce technology and screen time.* Just as we have learned about the need for lights to be dim to mimic the rhythms of nature, so too do we need to put down the screens to allow our mind and body to rest before we can sleep.
- *Slow the mind and body.* Engaging in somatic work (activities that centre you in your body) such as breathwork, meditation or gentle stretching can be a great way to relax and calm the mind and body before diving into bed and closing your eyes. So too are things such as reading or listening to calming music.

- *Put down your worries.* So many of us go to bed with our minds still racing (I too am guilty of this). Instead of laying in bed with thoughts keeping you up, putting these thoughts on paper can really help. Using a journal or writing a list are extremely powerful in being able to release thoughts, let them go and come back to them the next day. By putting your thoughts or worries on paper you can release them for the night, allowing you to fall asleep easier.

Again, this is about finding what works for you. There is no right or wrong, only things that do or don't work for you. It will require trial and error, and knowing that sometimes things will work, and other days you may need to do something different. As best you can, though, it's important to develop a consistent routine. This will help your mind and body learn the signs that signal sleep.

Rest

Rest is giving your mind, body and soul the opportunity to slow down, take it easy and be calm. Whether it's mindfulness activities, meditation, walking in nature, a lazy Sunday afternoon, taking a nap, hobbies and craft – however you choose to rest or be mindful allows your body to reconnect with itself and come back to its natural state.

Living in such a fast-paced society, and with teaching being so demanding and pulling us from one thing to another, we often neglect the desire and need to rest. It is hard to rest with to-do lists, lesson planning and marking that needs attending to, or when cleaning, washing and cooking also need to be done. However, if we don't find the time to rest, our wellbeing is impacted.

Engaging in rest or mindfulness activities can have significant benefits to our mind, body and soul, some of which are similar to exercising or having a great night's sleep. Resting or engaging in mindful activities can reduce stress and anxiety, boost our immune system, reenergise us, allow us to process our thoughts and clear our mind, and improve resilience. Mindfulness has also been shown to reduce work-related stress, decrease staff turnover and burnout, and increase job satisfaction and performance (Ackerman 2017).

Actively practising rest and mindfulness needs to be built into your everyday wellbeing strategy. Five to 10 minutes daily doing something restful or mindful is enough to experience some benefit, and far more effective than saving it up for the weekend or holidays. The small things matter as much as the big things and can accumulate to have a significant impact on your daily life. Give yourself permission to take five minutes (or more) out of your day to rest and do something mindful.

Your Non-Negotiables

While the idea of the Foundations for Optimal Energy Framework is to see each piece of the puzzle as essential to be able to function well and have optimal energy, functioning well does not always look the same nor is energy always equal. Some days we require more energy than others.

Part of knowing you have all the energy you need is being aware of what you have coming up the following day or week and making sure you have laid the foundations. It also means being aware of what your week looks like, both at work and home, and what might impact the energy you require, how you build energy and what takes from your energy. This means being aware of how much sleep you might need, what foods to eat and if you're drinking enough water.

To help with this, I like to ensure I have non-negotiables in my day that allow me to function at my best and ensure I look after my physical, mental and emotional wellbeing. Non-negotiables are things I commit to doing each day. Whether I am working, travelling or at home, these things are a must. I have even been known to plan a day out or a holiday around these things. For example, when I travel I book a hotel with a gym or park close by so I can move my body; if I know I am going to have a busy day at work I will make sure I prep meals so I don't have to worry about what to eat or not having enough time to make something; and I never leave the house without my water bottle. My non-negotiables are:
- Drink at least four litres of liquid a day (minimum two litres of water, the rest is usually tea and coffee).
- Move my body each day. Some days this is a gentle walk, others a run or weights session.

- Eat a variety of whole foods, balanced with other food I enjoy.
- Make time to breathe and/or meditate (rest and mindfulness).
- Get outdoors and be in nature.
- Read, create or learn (again, this is part of rest for me).
- Spend time with my partner and/or family.
- Reflect on my day and practise gratitude.

I encourage you to develop some non-negotiables just for you. These do not have to be big, and you do not have to do them all at once. I have built my non-negotiables over time and they change and adapt depending on what's happening in my life. I have also, as much as possible, built routines and habits to help support my non-negotiables. This includes being organised and prepared for what is happening in my week and making sure I have done what I need so things can happen smoothly, allowing my energy and function to be optimal.

For a long time now, I have put some time aside on weekends to prepare my food for the coming week (this has become somewhat of a weekend non-negotiable). I have also had many colleagues comment on my 'always healthy lunches'. While my meals may be nutritious and appear healthy, I don't eat them for that reason. I eat them because it helps me to maintain my energy, to function well and to get me through the day.

To be honest, what I eat is pretty boring; however, I know by eating these meals I will feel satisfied, and it will help my body and brain to function as the day goes on. I also don't want to go back to class after lunch with a food hangover from grabbing hot chips (which I love but save for when I am not working or needing to function well) or on a sugar high because I wasn't prepared and all I could find were snacks in the bottom drawer of my desk. This is an example of intentional action and non-negotiables that support energy and function.

To be honest, this is one of the reasons feel a little uncomfortable with morning teas being part of a staff wellbeing strategy, and so many strategies for staff wellbeing centering around food. The foods that are usually associated with these activities are not actually helpful to our physical wellbeing or energy, nor do they support us to function well.

I should also add here that it is actually not the morning tea itself that contributes to our wellbeing – it's just a vehicle to allow us to connect with our colleagues, the same as chocolates at the end of term are a sign of appreciation.

To be clear, I am not saying we should cancel all morning teas; I am, however, suggesting it may be time to reflect on how many of the wellbeing strategies we have are food-related, and if there are other ways we can find opportunities to connect or show appreciation in the workplace.

One essential factor to figuring out your puzzle pieces, knowing your non-negotiables and building your foundations for optimal functioning is knowing what each of the five areas of the framework looks like to you. Everyone will require different amounts of sleep and water; different foods work for different people; and we all rest, engage in mindfulness and move our bodies in different ways. None are right or wrong, as long as they allow you to achieve the energy you need and desire.

Your approach on a weekday may also look different to the weekend or holidays. While I prepare and eat my 'healthy meals' on a work day, weekends can look very different, as I know I don't require the same amount of energy or ability to function. Having a burger and hot chips on a Saturday for lunch, when my afternoon consists of not much and I don't need a huge amount of energy, is a perfect example of being aware of what food I need to allow me to function for what is happening in my day. I wouldn't be having a burger and hot chips if I was teaching afterwards, but on a weekend, it serves me well.

Relationship and Connection for Energy and Function

Along with the five areas in the Foundations for Optimal Energy Framework, there are other things that impact our energy levels and our ability to use energy. While the list of these things is pretty much endless, there is one I would like to draw your attention to: relationships.

Other people play a key role in our energy levels. I am sure you can think of someone who lifts you up and makes you feel energised, and someone who you find draining to be around. Working in teams with other people and living with others can cause our energy to rise or fall. When we surround ourselves with people who increase our energy, we naturally want to be with them more; however, we also need to learn to manage relationships we find draining.

A relationship that zaps a lot of energy from us does not always have to be a negative relationship. As teachers, at times our students can zap our energy. To ensure we can contribute to these relationships well, without always feeling depleted or low on energy, there are a few things we can do:

- *Receive and give.* Often we give, give and give, especially our time and energy. To allow your energy to be maintained, aim to do things for yourself, or let others help you.
- *Keep it light.* Play and having fun is a known way to help you relax and refill your energy as needed. Trying to keep things light, showing up with curiosity and working on connection before content (for example, asking 'How are you?' before 'Have you got today's lesson resource?') can help to maintain energy as you work with others.
- *Ask more questions.* Our brains love to fill the gap, and when we don't know the answer to something, it's clever at making something up. This can be difficult as we often view things through a negative bias, and when we are unsure or in conflict, our brain will fill our head with unhelpful stories. This can be extremely draining. One of the best ways to avoid this happening in our relationships is by asking more questions. You can try questions such as:
    - 'Can you help me understand what you mean by that?'
    - 'I am thinking that you want me to [action], is this correct?'
    - 'I am feeling confused/overwhelmed by [topic], can you help to [action]?'

By doing this we are allowing ourselves to get the right information from others and not waste energy making something up instead.

Chapter Summary

- Energy and function are connected to physical health: how we feel physically.
- The foundations to optimal energy include nutrition, movement, hydration, sleep and rest.
- What we need for optimal energy and function differs from person to person. Do what works for you.
- Being physically healthy and moving our body can help to reduce stress and overwhelm, increase energy levels, support us to think more clearly and increase productivity.
- Developing non-negotiables is a good way to build consistency and habits that support optimal energy and function.

From Theory to Action

Now you have permission to create your own approach to your physical wellness and what you need to function well and maintain optimal energy, it is time to build that approach. As you do this, keep in mind that your approach will look different to others, and all that matters is that what you do works for you. At this point in time you may not be quite sure how to answer the following questions or what works or doesn't work for you, so if needed take time to figure this out.

As you work through the following questions, don't feel the need to answer them all at once. You may like to do this over a period of a week or month so you can really reflect on what does or doesn't work for you and what you would like to include in your Optimal Energy Approach. You may also like to complete this exercise in a journal so you can add to it and refer to it over time.

Optimal energy and functioning well:
- What does functioning well look and feel like to you?
- How do you feel when you have optimal energy?
- What things do you do and say when you have optimal energy and are functioning well?
- When, where and why might this look different? (For example, on work days versus weekends.)

Nutrition:
- What foods make you feel good and allow you to function well?
- What foods enhance your energy?
- What foods negatively impact how you function?
- What foods reduce your energy levels?

Movement:
- What does movement or exercise look like to you?
- How do you feel when you move or exercise?
- How do you feel when you don't move or exercise?

Hydration:
- Do you drink enough water?
- How do you feel when you are well hydrated?
- How do you feel when you are not well hydrated?

Sleep:
- How much sleep do you need to function well?
- What is the minimum number of hours of sleep you can have per night before you feel drained of energy?
- Do you have a sleep routine to signal it is time to sleep? If not, could you develop one?
- Are you getting enough sleep? If not, what do you need to do to improve this?

Rest:
- What do rest and mindfulness look like to you?
- How easy do you find it to allow yourself this time?
- When could you include rest in your day?
- How does rest and mindfulness impact your energy and how you function?

Give yourself as much time as you need to answer the above questions and come back to them as often as you like. When you have worked through these questions you can begin to make some commitments to yourself to help build your Optimal Energy Approach.

You can record your commitments below or write them somewhere you can refer to as often as needed. These are also great to keep inside your diary or day planner.

My Optimal Energy Approach

My Commitments

Area	Commitment
Nutrition	
Movement	
Hydration	
Sleep	
Rest	

Congratulations! You have made some significant commitments to helping you feel energised and function well each day. You may even like to have some of these as your non-negotiables. As you work towards your Optimal Energy Approach becoming part of your daily life, know that you need to apply a certain level of flexibility with these things, as they are not always going to be exactly where you would like them to be. What you can do, though, is work on having as many puzzle pieces in place as you can. Every now and then, stop to congratulate yourself on all the pieces you have in place before life comes along and removes a piece of the puzzle temporarily.

My Non-Negotiables

After completing the tasks above, take some time to create a list of non-negotiables. These might not be things you can achieve straight away, but it is great to have something to strive towards. I don't always achieve my non-negotiable list 100%, but it is a great way to be clear on what I need to do each day to have the energy I need, and to be able to function well. Hopefully it does the same for you.

My non-negotiables are:

-

-

-

-

-

Chapter 5

Resilience

*Resilience is very different than being numb.
Resilience means you experience, you feel, you fail, you hurt. You fall.
But, you keep going.*
– Yasmin Mogahed

Resilience has been a very popular topic over the last few years, with school programs, books and workshops popping up everywhere. I have certainly had my own experience with resilience, starting with the idea that it was all about bouncing back. I now believe that resilience is far more connected with self-awareness, self-compassion and self-acceptance than just getting up when you fall.

For many years, including a lot of my childhood, any adversity I came across was met with the good old phrase 'just get over it'. This attitude to me is very close to the idea of 'just bouncing back', which I don't believe resilience is – we'll look at that a little later. To me, resilience is the ability to be aware of what is happening, see the events as they are, connect with my emotional state, regulate my emotions if needed, and allow myself the time and space to overcome what has occurred. It's about ensuring I honour my feelings and let them be, while also being proactive in moving forward. To me, resilience is not about 'getting over it' or 'moving on from it as quickly as I can'. Being resilient means fully stepping in – with your mind, body and soul – to what has happened, so you can be aware of what has occurred, and consciously be involved, through intentional decision-making and action, in what happens next.

Those of us who align with the idea that resilience is bouncing back are missing the opportunity to connect with what has happened and learn and grow from it. We need to learn how to actively engage in the steps of resilience, through awareness, engaging in adaptive coping strategies, and conscious decision-making and action (see figure 8). This allows us to not just learn and grow, but to ensure we are building these strategies like a muscle so we can apply them to any situation, big or small.

Figure 8: Three Steps to Building Resilience

Resilience is often thought of as something we need when we face adversity or challenge, yet the truth is, we need to be resilient and use adaptive coping strategies every day. Resilience is needed for both big and small occurrences: from an unexpected death to being stuck in traffic. While the intensity of these experiences are not the same they still require resilience so we can be aware of the event and our emotional state, engage in adaptive coping strategies, make conscious decisions and take meaningful action.

It took me a long time to realise that everyday resilience required this. I would often suppress and ignore less intense events or emotional experiences, telling myself they didn't matter – when in fact, each event and/or emotional response, regardless of intensity, requires resilience. 'Just getting over it' or 'positively thinking your way out' doesn't build resilience. The more we follow these three steps, for big and small events, the more we can naturally and easily work through things, and support both our everyday and workplace wellbeing. These three steps are also designed to help continually bring us back to our wellbeing point of equilibrium, our set point, where we feel most at home.

Often, we are required to use these steps when we are being pushed or pulled from our most natural state. Even though resilience is most commonly used for negative events, experiences and emotions, we may also need to work through these three steps if we are being pulled above our wellbeing equilibrium set point so we can make conscious decisions and take conscious action from a neutral state. Again, the more we actively engage in these things, the easier it is.

To bring this into our everyday life, and use these steps to sustain our wellbeing, we need to understand each of these areas – how they support each other, and how they support our wellbeing. Before we do that, though, let's establish a working definition of resilience so we know what we mean when we use this word.

What is Resilience?

Just like wellbeing, resilience has many different meanings, complexities and interpretations depending on who you ask and where you look. The Kids Help Line (2022) defines resilience as the ability to cope when things go wrong, however it also goes on to list seven other sub-definitions. Ackerman (2019) describes resilience as 'that ineffable quality that allows some people to be knocked down by life and come back stronger than ever. Rather than letting failure overcome them and drain their resolve, they find a way to rise from the ashes.' She goes further to explain that resilience can also be the quality of bouncing back. The *Britannica*

Dictionary defines resilience as 'the ability to become strong, healthy, or successful again after something bad happens' and gives the example, 'The rescue workers showed remarkable resilience in dealing with the difficult conditions' (Encyclopedia Britannica 2022).

These definitions, each including varying ideas, all suggest resilience has something to do with overcoming and coping when things go wrong – and that when people are knocked down or face something difficult, yet they recover quickly and come back stronger. Overall, we can surmise that resilience means successfully overcoming adversity or an obstacle.

We can also acknowledge that part of being resilient is the ability to recover; however, the term 'bounce back' doesn't quite feel right. Bouncing back implies we end up back where we started: something happens and we get up, dust ourselves off, bounce back to where we were and keep going. This doesn't align with the idea that through these challenges, we come back stronger. I like to think that every time something goes wrong, or we face a challenge or difficulty, we learn from it, grow, adapt and at times come back stronger. We do not bounce back to where we were before.

Another reason I struggle with the term 'bounce back' is that it suggests we dismiss the event, emotional experience, how we feel and what happened, and just keep going – continuing to put one foot in front of the other. To me, this doesn't feel right, either. There are lots of steps involved in being resilient. As we have seen, we need to acknowledge the event and our emotional state, engage in adaptive coping strategies, and make conscious decisions and take action. This can't happen if we just 'bounce back' to where we were before.

In fact, we might not even want to end up back where we were. Some of the biggest lessons in life and history have required resilience, yet haven't involved returning to how things were before. Through war, the making and sinking of the *Titanic*, even with Covid-19, we have been resilient. However, we have also grown, learned from these experiences, adapted, made changes and come back stronger, which is far more complex and challenging than simply bouncing back. Hence too why resilience is part of the work of wellbeing.

As we learn more about the work of wellbeing and how resilience supports it, I want to draw upon the following definition from the American Psychology Association: 'resilience is defined as the process of adapting well in the face of trauma or tragedy, threats or other significant sources of stress' (American Psychological Association 2020).

What I like about this definition is that it highlights our ability to adapt rather than just bounce back, and also brings in the concepts of trauma, tragedy, threats and significant stress, rather than just difficulties or challenges.

As wellbeing is not a one-size-fits-all approach, nor can the resilience strategies we have, use or engage in be. According to Genie Joseph, adjunct professor at Chaminade University in Hawaii, we draw upon three areas of resilience to help us cope: natural resilience, adaptive coping resilience and restored resilience (Riopel 2019). Natural resilience is the resilience we are born with – the resilience that comes naturally, our unique strength. Adaptive coping resilience is the resilience we have developed through experiencing challenges that cause us to grow stronger. Restored resilience is built by engaging in techniques that build lost resilience strategies. Techniques that build and increase restored resilience are focused around meditative and mindfulness techniques such as deep breathing, yoga or chanting. Neuroscientist and leading researcher Dr Richard Davidson (2019) suggests mindfulness as a strategy we can use to reduce stress and build resilience. He says as little as three minutes a day of mindfulness helps to build resilience.

Dr Davidson (2019) also believes that there are four components we need to focus on to promote resilience and wellbeing: awareness, connection, insight and purpose. He describes wellbeing as a skill that can be learned over time, with one of the key indicators of having higher wellbeing being the ability to recover more quickly. Hence, the more we work on our ability to become more resilient, the higher our wellbeing. He also suggests outlook, attention and generosity are the building blocks to positive wellbeing – yet another framework and approach to add to the growing list (Dr Davidson has conducted a significant amount of research which I recommend looking into if this area interests you).

The Four Types of Resilience

As with the definitions of wellbeing and resilience, there are also many viewpoints on the different types, components, skills and characteristics of resilience. A common view is that there are actually four types of resilience, which are said to encompass what's needed to be resilient in different situations. The four types are physical resilience, metal resilience, emotional resilience and social resilience (see figure 9).

Through my ongoing research, I've found the four types of resilience we'll look at here to be quite prominent and used by many in the field. I have chosen to include the four types of resilience as each relate to other areas of everyday and workplace wellbeing; they are easy to understand and differentiate; and each type comes with strategies that can be easily implemented individually and collectively. While there are four types of resilience we are going to explore, each is connected to the others, each is equal, and to be resilient in all areas of life, we need to understand and use each of the four types.

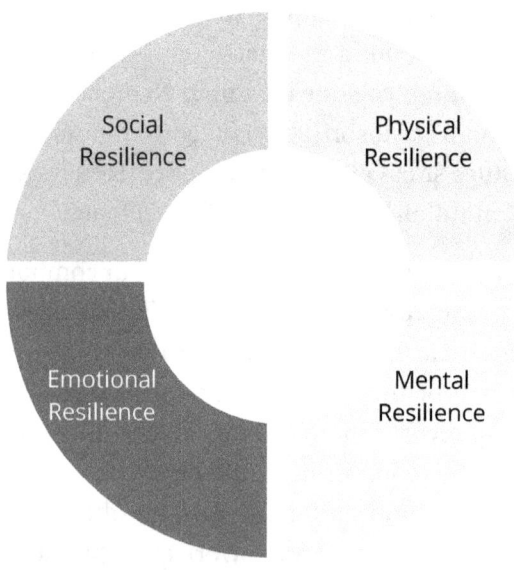

Figure 9: The Four Types of Resilience

Physical Resilience

Physical resilience is our body's ability to cope with and recover from physical pain, illness or excessive exertion. Good physical resilience is a sign you nourish and look after your body by focusing on nutrition, movement, hydration, sleep and rest, as we discussed in Chapter 4.

Physical resilience and physical health go hand in hand. It is important we recognise when we need to improve both our physical health and physical resilience; that by doing one, we naturally and effortlessly improve the other. Physical resilience is also tied to energy and function within everyday wellbeing. Through developing stronger physical resilience, and ensuring we actively work on elements that contribute to our physical health, we can reap the benefits that allow us to have better energy and function.

What is important to recognise here is that physical health is where most people start when they begin on a path to a healthier lifestyle, realise they need to work on their wellbeing, or want to feel better about their physical appearance. What is often neglected when people do this, however, is the understanding that to succeed in any area regarding a change with physical health, you have to engage in being physically resilient. A new exercise program will make your muscles sore, a new eating plan may be hard to follow, going to bed earlier and breaking the habit of staying up late can be difficult, but all these things get easier with time, and the benefits that go alongside them are worth it. While initially it may be difficult, hard or challenging, physical resilience means you understand this will be the case and that you know it will get easier over time. The more we persist, the more things become part of what we do all the time, no longer requiring the same level, if any, of physical resilience to keep going.

Mental Resilience

Mental resilience is our ability to use our brain to work through challenging thoughts or discomfort. It is also what's needed to overcome mental illness or mental health issues. Those with good mental resilience can problem-solve, think creatively and stay focused when faced with a challenge.

Mental resilience is required to help overcome any thoughts, beliefs or stories we may have that are challenging us and how we want to be and feel. Mental resilience is also closely linked to emotional resilience.

Mental resilience is required when we are to do hard things; when we need to create new assessment tasks, write units of work or come up with targeted and well-planned ways to differentiate lessons; when the curriculum changes and we have to review current plans and make changes to them. All of these challenges and changes, as valuable as they are, can be hard and require mental resilience. In fact, a lot of what we do within our teaching role requires a significant amount of mental resilience, because let's face it: things change, we are having to think and solve problems all the time and our mental load is continuously under pressure.

Because we are responding to student need as teachers, stressors come up no matter how well-planned we are – not to mention the other things that take us by surprise on a daily basis. Your teaching partner being away so you have to organise their lessons; a student forgetting their lunch so you have to find them something to eat (I have worked in schools without canteens and made sandwiches in my lunch break for students); a lunch duty being extended because the other teacher on duty doesn't turn up; having to sort out a fight on the playground, which means your class has to do 'silent reading' while you find out what happened, while you yourself are distracted by how hungry you are and the fact that you didn't get to go to the toilet, but that doesn't matter because once you sort out this issue, you have to go back to teaching your class for the next hour. A teacher's mental load is real.

I believe the mental load we face as teachers is one of the most significant in any job – so it's no wonder we feel tired, experience mental fatigue and brain fog, and find it hard to engage in any high-level conversation after school hours (which is interesting in itself as that is when most schools hold staff, team and planning meetings, and it's often the only time they can). It is also one of the reasons we feel like our wellbeing is significantly impacted by our work. Each day, no matter how organised, well-planned and ready we are for our students to learn, a small (or big, depending on where you work) part of us is always anticipating something else. What's next? What now? This too increases our propensity for fight, flight or freeze, meaning we are always on edge, wondering, waiting. This in turn impacts our nervous system, cortisol levels and the body's stress state. This is not a healthy place to be, and learning how to manage it, through things such as physical exercise, relaxation techniques, social support or seeking professional help, are paramount to helping manage the mental load we experience day to day.

Emotional Resilience

Emotional resilience is our ability to manage and cope with thoughts and feelings that arise. Those with good emotional resilience are aware of their emotions and feelings as they occur, particularly in negative circumstances, and can regulate these effectively.

Emotional resilience is a key part to managing overall wellbeing, and perhaps one of the most crucial. It is also by far one of the most complex. Our ability to regulate and be agile with our emotions, and not let them control us, is a huge concept to learn, understand and put into practice. So much so, the entire of Chapter 6 is dedicated to emotional regulation.

Emotional resilience is tied with emotional regulation, and again with mental resilience. As we learned earlier, a teacher's mental load impacts their wellbeing, with a key part of this being the impact mental load has on emotions. The more we feel our mental load is under pressure, the more stressed, anxious, unsupported and frustrated we may feel. All of these things are connected to our emotional state and require emotional resilience.

In Chapter 6 we will look more deeply at emotions: how they impact our overall wellbeing, the importance of developing emotional resilience, and the emotional regulation strategies we can use to not only help with our mental load, but improve our everyday and workplace wellbeing.

Social Resilience

Social resilience is our ability to cope with and manage changes in relationships and society. It is also our ability to connect with and support others. This could be family, friends or colleagues. Those with good social resilience understand that relationships and social situations change and that they are always evolving; they do not let these changes impact their long-term wellbeing.

Social resilience is a key component to teacher wellbeing. As teachers, we have no choice but to be social – with the students we teach, colleagues we work with, teams we work in, and parents and the wider community we have to engage with. Being social is part of the job. However, social resilience is a key area that many teachers are unfamiliar with.

In a school setting, social resilience requires us to understand that how we engage, work with, interact with and respond to colleagues contributes to our everyday and workplace wellbeing. We must be aware that in a school setting our social situations will change. Each year, and often in between, teaching teams will change, leadership teams will change, whole staff groups can change. We require a high level of social resilience, for our own benefit and that of others, including those we work with and our students.

Not all these changes are in our control. Sometimes we may choose to change schools, or our leadership team may request that we change year groups. No matter what happens, if the decision has been made with the best intentions, we must execute a high level of social resilience in order to adapt to new situations, work with new people, and continue to ensure our colleagues, teaching teams, students and school community get what they need.

Coping Strategies for Resilience

What we are trying to do with resilience is find quicker, healthier and more resourceful ways to come back to our point of equilibrium. One way to do this is to increase our ability to engage in adaptive coping strategies. Resilience strategies can either be adaptive or maladaptive, meaning they support or inhibit our resilience.

Adaptive coping strategies are things that support our ability to overcome challenges and continue to grow – for example, mindfulness techniques, problem-solving, awareness of emotions and seeking support. Maladaptive coping strategies do the opposite of this and hold us back – for example, blame, denial, suppression of emotions, gossip, substance abuse or avoidance.

However, our ability to engage in adaptive coping resilience strategies, and to be resilient, can also depend on if whether we have high or low resilience attributes. These are listed in table 5.

Low Resilience Attributes	High Resilience Attributes
Low self-esteem/self-confidence e.g. in our teaching, planning or assessment abilities.	Improved self-discipline and self-respect, self-esteem and self-confidence, and self-efficacy (you know and believe you are doing all you can).
Lack of care for things that contribute to energy and function (nutrition, hydration, sleep, movement, rest).	Actively working on areas that support everyday wellbeing, including energy and function and resilience.
Lack of awareness of emotions and emotional regulation strategies.	Better able to think clearly and openly, and manage emotions when working in teams and with others.
Limited ability to make well-thought-out decisions and solve problems, e.g. 'I don't know how to support all students to learn so I will just do this worksheet because it is easy and fun'.	More logical and rational in decision-making with well-thought-out reasoning, e.g. 'This resource is best because it supports the learning even though it is not as fun or easy as the other option'.
Lack of responsibility, avoidance, blame, denial or justification; often involved in and contributing to staff gossip; does not respond well to change or challenge.	Takes responsibility for behaviours, actions and decisions and commits to working through challenges, seeing them as new opportunities.

Low Resilience Attributes	High Resilience Attributes
Disengagement from social and other challenges, e.g. low engagement and lack of contribution to team or school-wide tasks.	Is more engaged in the workplace, fosters positive working relationships, works collaboratively and cohesively, has a high sense of belonging and seeks fairness.
Acts irrationally and doesn't consider consequences, e.g. feels overworked so doesn't do playground duty despite knowlingly leaving students unsupervised.	Is more self and socially aware, can be a role model to others and demonstrates leadership and mentoring skills; is someone who other teachers seek advice from.

Table 5: Low and High Resilience Attributes
(Source: Adapted from Tillott 2020)

The table reflects many attributes that connect to our subjective and psychological wellbeing and the wellbeing of mind, body and soul. The better our physical wellbeing, emotional wellbeing and mental wellbeing, the higher our resilience attributes. Our ability to be resilient is a combination of all aspects of our wellbeing, and is directly tied to the work of wellbeing we engage in.

When we reflect on these attributes and link them with adaptive and maladaptive coping strategies, we can begin to formulate subjective and psychological wellbeing strategies that support the building of resilience. Sometimes the strategies we need to engage in may be quick fixes, simply to boost our mood, whereas others may be long-term strategies to build and continually improve our resilience. Either way, we need to be mindful of the fact that the strategies we use are either adaptive (resourceful) or maladaptive (unresourceful). It can also be helpful to think of it like this: our adaptive coping strategies are positive, work for us and are resourceful, whereas our maladaptive coping strategies are negative, work against us and are unresourceful.

Let's take a look at some adaptive and maladaptive coping strategies for both subjective and psychological wellbeing (table 6).

	Subjective Wellbeing – Pleasure-Driven	Psychological Wellbeing – Fulfilment, Meaning, Purpose
Adaptive Coping Strategies	• Massage • Walk in nature • Connecting with friends or colleagues • Exercise • Seeking solutions and problem-solving	• Daily mindfulness • Reframing negative thoughts • Ongoing journalling and reflection • Learning from failure • Setting new goals
Maladaptive Coping Strategies	• Alcohol • Substance abuse • Gossip	• Continuous lack of responsibility, blame, denial, justification, excuses • Focusing on negative and spiralling thoughts

Table 6: Adaptive and Maladaptive Strategies for Subjective and Psychological Wellbeing

When we engage in the work of resilience, there are two main things we are responding to: the event itself, and our thoughts and emotions. These will vary in intensity, impact and urgency. The time, space and coping strategies needed to be able to come back to your point of wellbeing equilibrium will also differ depending on the situation.

It took me a little while to realise that my internal dialogue was as much a contributor to my wellbeing as what I did physically. With so much emphasis on wellbeing strategies being about the physical body, I can understand why. This is somewhat problematic in the space of the work of wellbeing. We are so consumed with focusing on physical wellbeing, we neglect and perhaps undervalue the mental and emotional space.

The mind/body connection is however very real. As Buddha said, 'What we think we become.' Our thoughts, our mindset, what we focus on, the stories we tell ourselves, our language – all of this contributes to our wellbeing, and in return requires the work of emotional and mental resilience. Our adaptive coping strategies to build resilience should be about balancing mind, body and soul, and working on all aspects of wellbeing.

For this, we need to understand that resilience, which we often think of as our ability to overcome an event, really is, as we learned earlier, about coping and managing things that cause us stress – which includes stress created through our thoughts and emotional states.

Stress caused by events that happen to us that are out of our control, or decisions we have made or action we have taken, are far easier to identify than stress caused by our thoughts (the stories we tell ourselves) or our emotional state. However, each of these can equally impact our wellbeing and each requires us to be aware, use adaptive coping strategies and follow with conscious actions and decisions to ensure we balance all areas of our wellbeing.

Let's take a look at some examples of events, thoughts and emotions that cause us stress (table 7).

Events that Might Happen	Thoughts we Might Have	Emotions we May Feel
Being the only teacher to move year levels at the start of a new year.	'Doesn't anyone in the team like me? I thought we were friends?'	Rejection
A student misbehaving and you not receiving help when you need it.	'Doesn't anyone at care about me?'	Anger
Teaching a lesson that doesn't go to plan.	'That lesson was awful, I am a terrible teacher'	Judgement
Turning up to a meeting late.	'I am so disorganised, I can't do anything right'	Self-doubt
A student yelling at you telling you you're a terrible teacher.	'My students don't like me, will they ever?'	Anxiety
A number of things added to your workload following a meeting.	'There is no way I can ever get this done'	Overwhelm

Table 7: Events, Thoughts and Emotions that Cause us Stress

While major events are most likely one-off occurrences, thoughts can linger and reappear. The more we engage in these negative thoughts, the more we inhibit our ability to be resilient and recover quickly. Instead, we should engage in strategies for mental and emotional resilience.

Being aware of the four types of resilience can help us to know what to draw upon when we find ourselves in situations where we need to overcome obstacles; however, we also need to be regularly engaging in a variety of strategies that build resilience, despite not having anything specific to overcome.

It is too little too late to build the strategy when you are in the situation. If you didn't train for the marathon, you can't make up for it on your way to the start line. The work we do to build resilience and to ensure we have the ability to cope when things don't go to plan can't always happen when we are in the middle of report writing, marking or planning for next term. We need to have already been engaging in resilience strategies, know what works and what doesn't, know what to apply when, and be aware enough to do these things as best we can before things get challenging. While this isn't possible for unexpected events, it is possible for things we can anticipate coming. Resilience should not only be like a bandage, used to hold broken bones together that snapped quickly, without warning, but also like the calcium we take or strength training we do to build density in our bones to avoid them breaking in the first place. Building and actively engaging in resilience strategies is both the prevention and the cure.

For many teachers, strategies for resilience need to be part of our everyday toolkit. We often work in high-stress periods and carry a lot on our plates. To build positive and effective resilience strategies, we should look to the four types of resilience: physical, mental, emotional and social. Doing this will ensure we have the strategies needed to build effective and easy-to-use resilience strategies that support everyday and workplace wellbeing. This is another example of mind, body and soul or mental, emotional and physical health and wellbeing.

As with all wellbeing concepts and strategies, the most important thing to remember is that we are trying to find what works for us. The resilience strategies we deploy through these four areas will be different for everyone and used and needed at different times. Wellbeing and resilience strategies are a bit like how teachers devour a box of Roses chocolates on the staffroom table. The caramel and fudge ones go first, with the orange and peppermint creams left until last. Do what works for you, what makes you feel good, and every now and then try something different.

Chapter Summary

- Resilience is the ability to manage, work through and overcome times of challenge, obstacles, trauma and stress.
- We need to learn to actively engage in the steps of resilience: awareness, adaptive coping strategies, and conscious decision-making and action.
- When faced with stress or challenges, we draw upon three areas of resilience to help us cope: natural resilience, adaptive coping resilience, and restored resilience.
- There are four types of resilience needed in different situations: physical resilience, metal resilience, emotional resilience and social resilience.
- Our ability to engage in adaptive coping resilience strategies, and to be resilient, can also depend on if we have high or low resilience attributes.

From Theory to Action

With resilience strategies being both the prevention and cure, we need to be actively engaging in the work of resilience at all times.

The table below includes some examples of things you may like to try to improve or enhance your resilience. You may notice some of the strategies listed are the same as strategies we looked at in Chapter 4 (Energy and Function), or that we will look at in Chapter 6 (Emotional Regulation). The ripples of wellbeing work, the crossover and the shared benefits are never-ending, but each is equally important.

Strategies for Resilience

Resilience Type	Resilience Strategies
Physical resilience *Time to get active.* *Physically active people are more resilient.*	• Add exercise into your weekly routine. • Ensure you are getting enough sleep. • Eat nutritious foods. • Spend time in nature.
Mental resilience *Mentally resilient people don't take things personally.*	• Acquire new skills if what you are doing is challenging. • Keep things in perspective; reframe negative thoughts or stories. • Take decisive action on things you can control.
Emotional resilience *Emotionally resilient people are aware of their emotions, but can still think clearly.*	• Be flexible and adapt how you think and respond to situations, events and thoughts. • Practise compassion, for yourself and others. • Practise gratitude, meditation and breathwork, and journalling to move and release emotional energy.
Social resilience *Socially resilient people get out and about with others to boost resilience.*	• Connect with family and friends often. • Find ways to laugh and play with others. • Seek social support when you are experiencing a more challenging time.

Using the suggested strategies above, create a plan to build more of these into your day and week. Some you can do easily and plan for, others will need to be tried and tested when you need to use that type of resilience.

Strategies I will try:

Physical resilience	
Mental resilience	
Emotional resilience	
Social resilience	

Chapter 6

Emotional Regulation

By teaching people to tune in to their emotions with intelligence and to expand their circles of caring, we can transform organizations from the inside out and make a positive difference in our world.
– Daniel Goleman

Being aware of, understanding, expressing and talking about emotions is still quite a new topic, and something both in our everyday and workplace environments we are learning to do more and more of.

Many of us grew up in a time where we were encouraged and expected to keep emotions hidden, to 'just get on with it' or to 'not let things bother you so much'. This has created a gap in our ability to not only recognise and understand how we feel, but also to be able to hold space for others to feel comfortable with, share and communicate their emotions.

This is partly because we have also been taught that emotions are good or bad, and that we should only show the good, happy, positive emotions.

'No one needs to see you cry', 'No one likes a sad face', 'Anger doesn't get you anywhere'. Does any of this sound familiar? Statements like this suggest that our emotions and how we feel are less important than how someone else who has to interact with us might feel.

Interestingly, alongside understanding and expressing emotion comes the ability to show and act with empathy, which is also now seen as a much-needed skill in the workplace. It's easy to see why we have been encouraged to walk around with masks on, to not acknowledge or connect with how we truly feel, to push down our emotional state, and even to not acknowledge our emotions at all. To do the opposite requires self-awareness, courage and vulnerability – some of the most challenging skills of all, and ones that we are still very much learning about.

Part of understanding our emotions and how these contribute to our overall wellbeing is learning to recognise and sit with our emotions, learning how they feel in our body and understanding how they affect us, yet many of us haven't been given the opportunity to do this. However, I have noticed that over time more people and schools are becoming willing to talk about emotions and feel more comfortable with their own and others' emotions.

Emotional awareness in the workplace, as a teacher, also comes with its own complexities. We often have to keep our happy faces on for most of the day. Teaching often requires us to keep going, push our own emotions aside, and show up for our students 100% regardless of what is going on. If we are having a bad day we can't just hide behind our desk, go out for a walk to clear our head, chat with a colleague while grabbing a coffee, or pretend to be working when in actual fact we are playing Tetris to distract ourselves from other issues. We have to keep going. We have students who constantly need teaching, attending to and connecting with, regardless of our emotions – we have to show up for them (I would like to note here that if at any point your emotional state impacts how you teach and interact with students, taking some time away from the classroom may be advised).

I can recall numerous times in my teaching career where I have had to push my own emotions aside to find the energy, calmness and 'good' emotions needed so I could carry on for my students. Feeling stressed about all the planning I needed to do, but having to let that go to teach a maths lesson on fractions; feeling annoyed that a team meeting was taken over by a colleague and we got nothing done, but having to put my frustration aside to teach in the afternoon; or feeling attacked by a parent who sent the most awful email without knowing all the details, and – while my stomach sank and I worried about what would happen – having to continue on reading the class novel and teaching literacy groups before I could share my side of the story with my principal.

These experiences are common in the teaching space, yet it doesn't make it any easier. The idea that we have to keep pushing on and pretend everything is fine until 3 pm not only means we need to know how to quickly and confidently be aware of, manage and regulate our emotions, but it also means our mental load becomes heavier. This has a significant impact on our wellbeing, and can cause problems if we don't deal with the issues causing these emotions in the first place.

There are multiple terms and phrases used in the space of emotions, including emotional regulation, emotional intelligence, emotional awareness and emotional agility. Each of these terms is important as we learn about our emotions as a key contributor to wellbeing. As you begin to learn more about emotions and how they impact both your subjective and psychological state, you may find these terms used interchangeably – so let's find out what they mean (see table 8).

Terminology	Definition
Emotional regulation (sometimes called emotional management)	The process of influencing which emotions you have, when you have them, and how you experience and express your feelings. It can be automatic or controlled, conscious or unconscious (Gross 1998, cited in Chowdhury 2019).
Emotional intelligence	Awareness of your own emotions and moods and those of others, especially in managing people (Collins 2022).

Terminology	Definition
Emotional awareness	The ability to recognise your own and others' emotions; very much linked to emotional intelligence.
Emotional agility	The ability to accept and notice your inner world – your thoughts, emotions and stories – viewing even the most powerful ones with compassion and curiosity (David 2016).

Table 8: Definitions of Emotion-Related Terms

Regardless of which area you focus on, learn about or implement, they are all designed to help you become more aware of, understand, better manage and regulate your emotions, and in return improve your state of wellbeing. Having a deeper understanding of emotions, including your own and others', can also impact workplace wellbeing. Daniel Goleman's work on emotional intelligence has helped us to understand that through developing this in the workplace we can create a more positive culture and increase productivity and performance.

Along with understanding our emotions comes understanding feelings. These two words are often used interchangeably, and while they may go hand in hand, they are not the same thing. Emotions and feelings are actually quite different, in that one is a physical response, and one is a mental response. Our emotions are said to be the physical response in our body, but feelings are the mental descriptions and words we attach to the emotions. The emotions we experience are usually quick and instant; whereas a feeling is a longer-term response, can look different from person to person, and we may stay feeling a certain way longer than the emotion lasts. Alongside this is also the story and meaning we attach to the experience. As neuroscientist António Damásio said, 'We are not thinking machines that feel, we are feeling machines that think.'

As teachers trying to improve both our everyday and workplace wellbeing, we need to become aware of our emotions, feelings and the stories that go alongside them, as these all impact wellbeing significantly on a day-to-day, moment-by-moment basis.

Five Steps to Emotions for Positive Wellbeing

Have you ever been left alone with your thoughts? It is amazing what your mind can do unsupervised. We can easily turn an emotion into a feeling, and a feeling into a story, and within minutes let it spiral out of control like a bad movie being played out in our mind.

Here is a scenario you may be familiar with: your teaching partner isn't their usual self, and doesn't say good morning as they normally would. This makes you feel sick in your stomach (emotion), which in turn makes you feel hurt and has you worried that you have done something wrong (feeling). Rather than ask if everything is okay, you tell yourself they must be annoyed at you after yesterday's staff meeting (story and meaning), when in actual fact you have no idea what's going on. However, because you don't want to upset them further, you go and ask your other teaching partner who shares their opinion (more story) and from here it builds and builds and builds – when in fact all that happened was that your teaching partner was grumpy because they got stuck in traffic.

While this might seem like a long, fabricated example, things like this happen all the time. Whether it is with a teaching partner, a parent or during a staff meeting, we constantly experience emotions and feelings, and unless we are comfortable with asking questions and finding out what is going on, we fill the space with story and meaning that may or may not be true. This is not a positive place to be, and over time this behaviour starts to impact our overall wellbeing. In order to master our emotions, manage them and ensure our emotional state positively impacts our wellbeing, there are five steps I recommend teachers work on individually and collectively (see figure 10 overleaf).

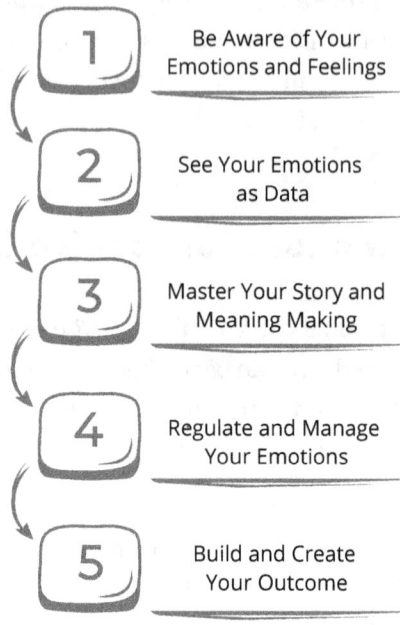

Figure 10: Five Steps to Emotions for Positive Wellbeing

Be Aware of your Emotions and Feelings

Notice how you feel and build your vocabulary around emotions and feelings

The first step is becoming aware of how we feel. This means we have to become comfortable with tapping into what our body is telling us, letting the emotions and feelings come and go, and being okay with listening to these things. We also need to be self-aware enough to know that some emotions will make us feel good, and others not so much. Self-awareness is about recognising all emotions, and not feeling the need or desire to ignore an emotion because of how it makes us feel, or how we perceive others may feel. Each emotion is as valid as another, and through self-awareness we can recognise the importance of knowing, naming and understanding these and what they mean for us.

Self-awareness and being aware of our emotions gives us the power to be able to control our emotions, rather than letting them control us. According to Daniel Goleman, 'If your emotional abilities aren't in hand, if you don't have self-awareness, if you are not able to manage your distressing emotions, if you can't have empathy and have effective relationships, then no matter how smart you are, you are not going to get very far' (Goleman 2005).

To have strong emotional awareness, we must be able to identify, name and put language around our emotions so as to manage and regulate them. To do this, we need to ensure we have an expansive and extensive emotional vocabulary and are able to be granular in the way we describe and talk about our emotions.

What we put language around, we experience. This means the more limited our vocabulary, the more limited our experience, and vice-versa. To fully understand our emotions, how we feel, what we are experiencing and what we want to experience, we have to be able to expand our vocabulary. In *Atlas of the Heart*, Brené Brown (2021) unpacks 87 emotions and experiences that are part of being human; yet she also reports that many of us only use three words to describe our emotions: happy, sad and angry. If we can only experience what we put language around, expanding our vocabulary beyond happy, sad and angry is an important concept to master.

Along with knowing and naming emotions, Susan David (2016), author of *Emotional Agility*, highlights the importance of becoming granular with your emotions. Emotional granularity is your ability to be succinct and specific with your emotions and how you feel; to become curious and acknowledge what is really happening for you; and to be clear on the words you use to describe what you are experiencing and how you feel. The better we are at doing this, the more we are able to seek to understand ourselves and others, learn and grow from what is happening, and respond to experiences and events in meaningful ways that move us forward.

Expanding our own emotional vocabulary is not only important for ourselves, but also for how we connect with others, including our students and colleagues. By developing a deeper understanding of emotions and feelings, we can identify these in others more easily, help them to understand how they may be feeling themselves, and act with more empathy and compassion. Moving beyond happy, sad and angry as the most common three emotions we are able to build more positive relationships with ourselves, our students and our colleagues.

There are great tools and graphics out there to help understand emotional vocabulary. I highly recommend checking out Brené Brown's list of emotions in *Atlas of the Heart*, Susan David's Emotional Granularity checklist (David 2021) or one of the many emotion wheels that exist based on the work of psychologist Robert Plutchik (a quick google image search will see you with plenty of options).

See Your Emotions as Data

Understand emotions and feelings are not good or bad, they just are

When we talk about emotions, we use words such as good, bad, positive or negative to help describe how we feel, and also as a way to organise emotions into different categories. But are emotions and feelings really good or bad, positive or negative? I like to think not. All emotions are equally valid, are just as worthy as one another, and each deserves to be felt and understood.

Many of us have been led to believe that good or happy emotions are better than other emotions, and that anything that makes us feel bad or negative should be replaced quickly with happy thoughts. This is not actually helpful. Firstly, this creates what is commonly known as toxic positivity; and secondly, this also means we are suppressing emotions, which over time can negatively impact our wellbeing in other ways.

Toxic positivity is the belief that we should only engage in positive and happy thoughts, especially when experiencing a difficult or challenging time. This is not a healthy approach to emotional management or regulation, and can cause people to deny how they really feel. This can also create shame or guilt over what are perceived to be negative emotions, for example anger, grief or frustration. When we tell someone to 'just think happy thoughts' or 'look on the bright side', not only are we denying how they truly feel, we are also encouraging them to suppress their emotions and negating the opportunity for authentic human connection.

When we suppress emotions, we are denying or ignoring what exists. This could be because we have been led to believe that we should not feel negative or bad emotions, or because we don't want to face what has actually occurred. Suppressing emotions can also be a mask we wear when we don't want to acknowledge that something isn't working, when we have made a mistake or when we need help.

Teachers can at times suppress emotions due to 'not wanting to cause a fuss', because they don't want to make more work for someone else, or because they are afraid to appear like they don't know what they are doing. This can also reinforce a cycle of toxic positivity. Rather than allowing this to occur, as teachers, in teams and as a whole school, we have to become comfortable with allowing people to express and share their emotions. Failure to do so may impact all six areas of everyday and workplace wellbeing and contribute to a negative school culture.

So, if emotions and feelings are not good or bad, positive or negative, what are they?

Emotions are simply data – data that our body is sharing with us to let us know we feel a certain way. Feelings come about when we attach meaning to the emotions. None are good, bad, positive or negative; emotions and feelings just are. What matters, however, is how we respond to the emotion and feeling we experience.

Emotions and feelings come with a certain energy and intensity. It is what we do with this energy and intensity that can make the emotion or feeling good or bad. Feeling angry is a completely normal human emotion, as is feeling frustrated, annoyed or disappointed. What we need to be aware of though is how we respond or react to how we are feeling. Feeling angry that a colleague hasn't done their share of planning and now you have to pick up the slack is an acceptable emotional response; turning that anger into yelling and screaming at them isn't. Being upset that you have to move year group next year when you don't want to is an acceptable emotional response; telling your principal that they need to keep you where you are or you will move school is not. Being frustrated at the immense number of parent emails you receive is an acceptable emotional response; ignoring the emails and not responding is not.

It is not the emotion or feeling that is good or bad, positive or negative, it is what you do with the energy it creates and how you react or respond.

Master Your Story and Meaning Making

Be mindful of your stories and the meaning you make

Along with emotions and feelings comes story and meaning. As shared earlier, we attach meaning and story to everything, whether it's true or not. The story and meaning we make can impact how we interpret, respond or react to a situation. Therefore, we need to be aware of the story and meaning we make, especially if it is just that – a story with no truth attached. Part of the difficulty with this is that our brain, the story and meaning maker, is quick. It is so quick that we don't even realise or see the story it has made up.

Meaning making is the process we go through when we interpret events, situations, experiences, relationships and ourselves. Put simply, something happens, we attach meaning and we react or respond accordingly.

How we make meaning depends on a significant number of other factors that are part of our filtering system. How we filter and interpret events or situations impact how we uniquely see the world and create our own reality. When we experience an event or situation, there are thousands, if not more, pieces of information going into our brain at once. So as not to overwhelm us, and so we can focus on what matters and the information we need, our brain must very quickly decide what information to delete, distort and generalise. This happens in a multitude of ways including through our five senses, as well as considering our beliefs, values, past experiences, expectations, biases, culture, preferences and so on. As mentioned, this happens so quickly we don't even realise it; and if we did see what was going on at that granular level for every piece of information, we would be so exhausted that we wouldn't be able to do anything else.

This is also why two people can experience the same situation, yet have completely different experiences, viewpoints, reactions and responses. Our ability to filter and process information, then delete, distort or generalise based on our own filtering system, is why one teacher can be stressed at the mention of a school assembly item and the other not. It's why two teachers can walk away with a very different understanding of what is expected of them, despite sitting in the same staff meeting; or why two teachers can overhear a student argument, yet have different opinions about what was going on. How we filter the world is unique to us, and will impact our emotional response, feelings and meaning we make.

Once we understand this, we can begin to see why the meaning we make is crucial to managing and regulating our emotions. It is very much the meaning you make that can influence how you feel, and how you think long-term.

The interesting thing about meaning making is that we are never stuck with the meaning we first make. We can change the meaning we attach to something time and time again.

For example, if you think back to the scenario earlier in the chapter of a colleague coming to work unhappy, the meaning making that occurred through the thinking attached to the feeling was that they must be annoyed at you. However, there are infinite options and meanings we could attach as to why a colleague may not be their happy self: they may have had a bad night's sleep, slept through their alarm, had an argument with their partner, spilt their coffee on the way out the door, had unexpected family news, or just be having an off day. There is no way to know unless we ask, but because we are the meaning-making machines that we are, we jump to conclusions rather than seeking the truth.

When an experience, event or situation happens, don't jump to conclusions or fall into the trap of making meaning without consideration. Be curious, ask questions and play with different ideas about what something could actually mean. As Stephen Covey (2004) says in *The 7 Habits of Highly Effective People*, 'Seek first to understand'.

Regulate and Manage Your Emotions

Find a way to come back to neutral

Once we have considered the meaning we are making, or sought out the truth, we can then look to see if we are reacting or responding based on our emotions and feelings. How we react or respond will determine the outcome that follows, but again, as this happens so quickly, we often don't realise this is what is happening.

It is very easy to find yourself in a situation with emotions running wild, without having thought through each step along the way. As seen in the examples shared earlier, if we don't check in with our emotions and learn to regulate them, we may find ourselves yelling at colleagues, presenting our principal with an ultimatum or not engaging with parents. These are examples of what can go wrong if you don't learn to recognise and regulate your emotions.

When regulating and managing emotions there are a number of helpful strategies to use. I would like to reiterate here that the idea of snapping out of it or thinking happy thoughts is not the strategy we want to use or advocate for. As we know, all emotions are valid and matter; they each provide us with valuable data we need to pay attention to. However, that doesn't mean we need to react without thinking.

To regulate or manage our emotions, we first need to recognise how we are feeling. This is the ability to bring self-awareness to how you are feeling and ask yourself, 'What emotion am I experiencing right now?', followed by, 'How is this making me feel?'. Once you know this, you will be able to consciously choose your next step.

With some emotions impacting not just how we feel, but also how we think, it may be necessary to practise some mindfulness before acting. If we are in a certain emotional state – for example, feeling angry, frustrated or annoyed, or even tired or bored – we are less likely to be able to think openly, clearly and rationally. Using mindfulness is a great way to be able to calm and regulate your emotions, or break your state so you can come back to what's really going on and move forward with a clear frame of mind. You may like to use breathing strategies, go for a walk, listen to some calming music or spend time in nature. These strategies will most likely be similar to your resilience strategies that you worked on in Chapter 5.

Once we know our emotional state and how we feel, and have used some mindfulness if needed, we are then more able to regulate and manage our emotions. Other strategies for emotional regulation and management include practising self-compassion, engaging in self-care activities or seeking support. These strategies, along with pressing pause and giving people time and space when working through something difficult or challenging, are also useful in group and team settings.

Ultimately, the goal with emotional regulation and management is not to switch from sad to happy or negative to positive, but to become aware of your emotions, label them, check in with how they make you feel and give yourself the time and space needed so you can respond accordingly to create the outcome you desire.

Create and Build Your Outcome

Are you reacting or responding?

The reason we want to regulate our emotions and practise strategies for emotional management is so we can think through how we can respond to create the outcome we desire. While we can't control every outcome for every situation, we can come back to a place of feeling emotionally calm to allow ourselves to act with kindness, think logically and do what is best for ourselves and others.

If we aren't aware of our emotions, and the emotions and feelings we experience take over, we can find ourselves reacting to a situation rather than responding. A reaction is when we respond quickly to something – unconsciously, without thinking and based on our beliefs, values, circumstances and how we filter the world. A response is a more well-thought-out action – it takes longer, is conscious and allows us to weigh up different options.

While we don't need to think through every response, it is important to do so if our emotions have taken over and our natural response will not serve ourselves or others. Reacting is at times needed if we are in danger, such as about to have a car accident, or even in day-to-day conversation. When we react in situations like this and make decisions quickly, for the most part, everything is okay. However, when our emotions run high, reacting doesn't always serve us. This is where learning to pause and use mindfulness or another strategy can help us to think through what may happen if we continue to react. It also allows us to consider what it might look like if we slowed down before responding.

Feeling heated in a staff meeting? Taking a walk, a few deep breaths or coming back to the topic tomorrow could be the difference between saying something you don't really mean and being able to have a more professional conversation. Feeling overwhelmed by all the parent emails? Sorting through these, drafting responses and rereading them before sending could mean the difference between thoughtful responses and quick, short responses that require more work in the long run.

We need to be aware of and mindful of our emotions as part of the work of wellbeing. This is both an individual and collective effort. We need to be self-aware, and manage and regulate our emotions, but we also need to ensure our colleagues, teams and staff feel supported enough to be able to share when they are feeling uncomfortable, need a moment to think and find calm, or perhaps come back to the issue another time. If we build this as part of our culture, we are allowing teachers to feel safe in their emotions, to share and support others, and to act with empathy. From this space we can develop a better understanding of self and others and work towards a collective goal to improve everyday and workplace wellbeing for all.

Chapter Summary

- Emotions are not good or bad, positive or negative. They just are.
- Emotions are data.
- We most commonly use three words to describe how we feel: happy, sad and angry. However there are many other more nuanced ways to describe emotions and feelings.
- Emotions come with energy and intensity; it is what we do with the energy and intensity that can make the response good or bad, positive or negative.
- Emotional regulation helps us to be aware of and manage our emotions so we can react and respond more mindfully.

From Theory to Action

Now you know and understand the five steps to take to ensure your emotions positively impact your wellbeing, let's take a look at some practical strategies that can help to support the use of these each day.

Five Steps to Emotions for Positive Wellbeing	The Practical Piece
1. **Be aware of your emotions and feelings.** Notice how you feel and build your vocabulary around emotions and feelings	<ul><li>Pay attention to the physical signs your body displays for different emotions.</li><li>Be aware of the words you use most often to describe how you feel and build on these words to become more granular.</li><li>Build connection with others through talking about your own emotions and feelings and offering them the opportunity to do the same.</li></ul>

Five Steps to Emotions for Positive Wellbeing	The Practical Piece
2. **See your emotions as data.** Understand emotions and feelings are not good or bad, they just are.	• When an emotion arises, let it be, and don't think of it as good or bad, positive or negative. • Be curious. Ask yourself, 'What might my body be trying to tell me about this situation or event?' • Pay attention to the energy and intensity of the emotion and try not to let it overtake you.

3. **Master your story and meaning making.** Be mindful of your stories and the meaning you make.	• Ask yourself the following questions:
	  • 'What am I making this mean?'
	  • 'Is this true?'
	  • 'What else could it mean? What else could I tell myself instead?'

4. **Regulate and manage your emotions.** Find a way to come back to neutral.	• Ask yourself, 'How do I want to feel right now?' • Seek support or guidance if needed. • Use one of the regulation strategies to bring yourself back to neutral.
5. **Create and build your outcome.** Are you reacting or responding?	• Step back from the situation and consider if you are reacting from an emotional space or responding from a logical space. • Give yourself time between regulating your emotions and responding. • Consider different ways you could respond before taking action.

As easy as these strategies may look, they do require work. Remember, your brain is quick which means you may already have reacted or responded without really, if at all, thinking it through. You may also fall back into the trap of thinking some emotions are good or bad, or using the same three words to describe how you feel. This is okay, as long as you are working on making small changes each time you can. As with all components that make up the work of wellbeing, it takes time, patience and compassion.

Part 3

Where to from Here?

Now we know what wellbeing is, the difference between workplace and everyday wellbeing, and understand the work behind starting this journey, I am sure you have a few questions ...

What now?
What should I do?
What can schools do?

To wrap up a rather complex topic, we are going to learn how, by establishing self-efficacy and collective efficacy, we can decide on and apply transferable and practical strategies and themes that help increase everyday and workplace wellbeing.

We know that it is the responsibility of both the individual and collective to make change. To achieve long-term sustainable results, and move away from one-off band-aid solutions, we need to look at self-efficacy and collective efficacy, and see these as the real pillars to the change we seek.

Efficacy is the ability to produce or create an effect or outcome, or to achieve a desired result. This is exactly what we need to do to improve teacher wellbeing – achieve a desired result. If our goal is to achieve an outcome and have an impact, simply doing things is not enough. We have to believe that what we are trying to achieve is possible and that we can actually do it. This is known as self-efficacy.

Self-efficacy is the belief that you can complete a certain task successfully. In the space of wellbeing, self-efficacy plays a significant role in changing how we feel, think and do things. Without belief, the strategy doesn't matter.

Not only do we need to have self-efficacy – to believe that we can improve our own wellbeing – we also need to believe that the teams we work in and the whole school community can make these changes as well. Together, we must believe we can work on our everyday and workplace wellbeing, and that when we do this it will change how we feel, how much time we have, how productive and engaged we are, how well we work together, how happy we feel and more. We have to believe that we can make a difference to our wellbeing and the wellbeing of others. This shared belief is known as collective efficacy. You may be familiar with the term 'collective teacher efficacy'; it's when 'educators [in schools] believe in their combined ability to influence student outcomes', leading to 'significantly higher levels of academic achievement' (Bandura 1993).

The same idea of collective efficacy needs to be applied to teacher wellbeing. For teacher wellbeing to improve, we need to believe that our combined efforts will improve the wellbeing of ourselves, our colleagues and all educators, both in and out of the school and classroom. Once that is established, we can agree and unite on the work that needs to be done. It's not just a matter of how or what, but also a matter of who – and the who must be us.

We know there are multiple things that need to change at a system level, and yes, we are all hopeful this will come, and soon. As we explored in previous chapters, we are seeing teachers leave the profession in droves and the teacher shortage is real. Some leave teaching because they can't go on anymore, for whatever reason that may be, and we must respect that. No teacher leaves the profession easily, and I believe each teacher grieves for the students they will never meet, and the lessons they will never get to teach, because the job they dreamed of doing for years to come didn't turn out the way they planned.

For those of us who choose to stay, who choose to teach, and do all that comes with it, self-efficacy and collective efficacy are key. We must believe we can make a difference, and we can.

Through looking at everyday and workplace wellbeing, we can see the areas we need to focus on and that will support us the most. Along with this, however, are a number of key areas and topics that will also help to improve teacher wellbeing both at an individual and collective level. In Chapter 7, the first chapter of Part 3, we are going to look at how individual and collective efficacy can support teacher wellbeing; and in the final two chapters of this book – Chapters 8 and 9 – we will look at five key areas for teachers, and five key areas for schools, that can be addressed to support everyday and workplace wellbeing. These 10 areas combined, listed in table 9, will help to bring about the strategies needed and impact desired to improve teacher wellbeing.

What Can I Do? Practical Strategies for Teachers	What Can We Do? Practical Strategies for Schools
Building positive emotions	Building positive relationships
Taking responsibility	Setting a clear vision with supportive goals
Practising self-compassion	Utilising staff strengths
Setting boundaries	Having strong infrastructure
Creating sustainable habits	Fostering flexibility

Table 9: Practical Strategies for Teachers and Schools

Focusing on the above 10 areas, while developing self-efficacy and collective efficacy and using the framework throughout this book, will equip you to begin to make changes to your own wellbeing and that of others. I really do believe we can influence and impact the teacher wellbeing space. Do you?

Chapter 7

The Power of Efficacy

*A team is not a group of people that work together.
A team is a group of people that trust each other.*
– Simon Sinek

Efficacy for ourselves, and the teams we work in, matters. But what does efficacy really mean, and how does it link to teacher wellbeing?

To build our wellbeing, we have to believe we can do the work and that it will make a difference. Once we know what is wrong or what isn't working, where we want to be and what the desired outcome is, we can start to think about how – and then ask ourselves, do we believe this is possible? Not only is this important as it allows us to think through what's involved and to connect it to our reality, our circumstances and our resources, but it also emphasises the importance of connecting with our ability and desire to make the change we seek.

Knowing if you can actually do what's needed can at times be the first hurdle to overcome. 'Can I do this?', 'How will I do this?' and 'Do I have what I need to be able to do this?' are all common questions we ask or consider. Knowing if we can do what's needed considering our knowledge and ability or energy and effort, comes into play. This is often referred to as skill and will (see figure 11).

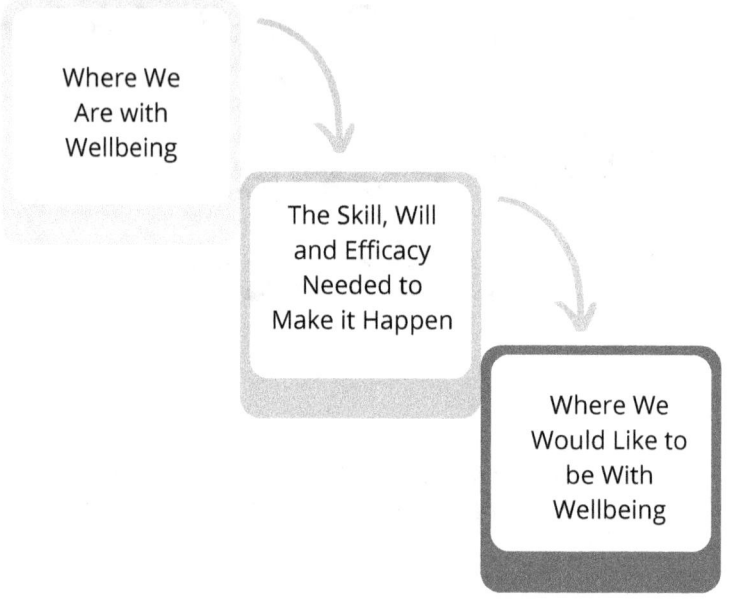

Figure 11: Skill, Will and Efficacy

Skill is underpinned by our expertise, knowledge, experience and ability to complete a certain task, whereas will is our attitude, confidence, feelings and desire to make it happen. To have the self-efficacy and collective efficacy needed for teacher wellbeing to improve, we also need to have both the skill and will to make it happen. Skill and will matter alongside efficacy.

Before we dive into both self and collective efficacy, let's take some time to further understand the concept of skill and will and how this can help us enhance efficacy and improve teacher wellbeing.

In a classroom setting we often need to draw upon our skill, will and efficacy to enhance student learning. We have all come across students who, at times, have had difficulty learning. To support them, we have spent time with and built relationships with them, differentiated learning, created tasks to meet them at their point of need and collaborated with colleagues to ensure they get exactly what they need. This is a great example of how skill, will and collective efficacy go together. Your *skill* of being an expert teacher in this area means you can differentiate and adapt learning as needed; your *will* means you have developed a positive relationship with your student and spent time with them; and the collective efficacy from you and your colleagues means you believed you could make a difference, hence the actions you took had more impact.

The opposite of this would see the student not making any progress at all. If you didn't have the skill, you wouldn't be able to adjust learning as needed; if you didn't have the will, you wouldn't make time for them; and if you didn't have the collective efficacy, you wouldn't believe the time and energy needed to support that student was worth it, so you wouldn't make it happen.

It is easy to see how these three things work together for student learning, but what about for our wellbeing and the wellbeing of our colleagues and staff? How do we apply these things to our everyday and workplace wellbeing? Let's think back to what is needed for improved workplace wellbeing: engagement, productivity and performance and growth. As teams and whole schools, we need to be prepared to look at, evaluate and change the systems, structures and processes behind these things. The same goes for everyday wellbeing. To do this well, we need high skill and high will (see figure 12 overleaf).

		Low	High
Will	**High**	'I don't know what to do but I want to do something.' This person really wants to help, has motivation and enthusiasm, but not the competency or knowledge. They need upskilling.	'I know what to do, I know how to do it and I want to do it.' This person has the competency, knowledge, motivation and enthusiasm. They are great when it comes to supporting others and leading the work.
	Low	'I don't know what to do and I don't want to do anything.' This person does not have the competency or knowledge. It may also not be a concern or issue for them.	'I know what to do, but I don't want to do it.' This person has the competency and knowledge but not the motivation or enthusiasm.
		Skill	
		Low	High

Figure 12: Skill and Will Matrix for Teacher Wellbeing

Figure 12 shows how skill and will can impact our ability to improve everyday and workplace wellbeing. It's based on the original skill and will matrix within the model of situational leadership created by Paul Hersey and Ken Blanchard in the 1970s. By using the skill and will matrix, you can also identify what areas you need to build and focus on when you look to improve certain wellbeing areas. Take a moment to plot yourself on this matrix. Are you high in will but low in skill, high in both will and skill, or maybe high in skill but low in will? What is it that you need to become high in skill and will? This, along with self-efficacy and collective efficacy, is part of the *how* of wellbeing.

In previous chapters we explored the work of wellbeing, which may have expanded your area of skill and perhaps will also. To bring this all together we'll take a closer look now at self-efficacy and collective efficacy, which will again build your skill and will.

What is Self-Efficacy?

Our understanding of self-efficacy is to be credited to the work of Albert Bandura. Bandura was a leading academic who, among many other things, helped psychologists understand that humans have the ability to adapt and self-regulate to achieve our desired future, meaning we are agents of our own self-development (Moore 2016). This theory was significantly influential in how we understand the human brain and human behaviour, and challenged many existing beliefs at the time.

Self-efficacy consists not only of our belief (if we think we can do something or not), but also our willingness to put in effort, our resilience when we face challenges, and whether we believe the results will be good. Self-efficacy must underpin the work we do on our own wellbeing, through the three main areas of everyday and workplace wellbeing – as we begin to identify what we want to change, what we need to do and which habits, strategies or steps we need to take. We have to believe we can do it, know it is worth it, put in the work and be willing to keep trying when we face setbacks.

When we have high self-efficacy, our ability to persist, have confidence and work through challenges is much greater than if we have low self-efficacy. Low self-efficacy stops us from beginning in the first place; it makes us feel like we can't make a change, or be uncertain about our decisions and actions. Self-efficacy also influences our view on the world. People with high self-efficacy are said to believe they have more control over their outcomes and what they experience – which is linked closely to having internal locus of control – whereas people with low self-efficacy believe that things happen to them and are out of their control – linked closely to having an external locus of control. Table 10 overleaf lists some of the traits of self-efficacy and locus of control.

High Self-Efficacy and Internal Locus of Control	Low Self-Efficacy and External Locus of Control
• Confident • Overcomes obstacles • Persistent • Believes things are in their control • Belief in ability to achieve things • Sets goals and strives • More positive emotions • 'I create my experiences'	• Low confidence • Gives up easily • Doesn't try • Believes things happen to them • Doesn't think things can change • Leaves things to fate • More negative emotions • 'Experiences happen to me'

Table 10: Self-Efficacy and Locus of Control

In all the work that exists in the wellbeing space right now, there is something missing in the messaging: the understanding that you need to believe you can do it and know that it is worth it. This is why so many people don't know what to do or how to do it, or give up when faced with a challenge, obstacle or the need to persevere. When you embark on your own wellbeing journey you must find the self-efficacy needed to make the change you desire.

Improving wellbeing is work. It requires having goals and changing habits, the way you have been doing things and 'the way it's always been done'. It also requires a level of grit, determination, perseverance and belief that you can make it happen; a combination of skill and will, self-efficacy and internal locus of control.

What makes self-efficacy so helpful is that it is not set – it isn't a trait that some have and others don't. Anyone can build, grow and expand their self-efficacy. The more you build self-efficacy, the more it grows. Imagine it like a cycle; you work on building self-efficacy, self-efficacy grows, you work on building self-efficacy, self-efficacy grows (see figure 13).

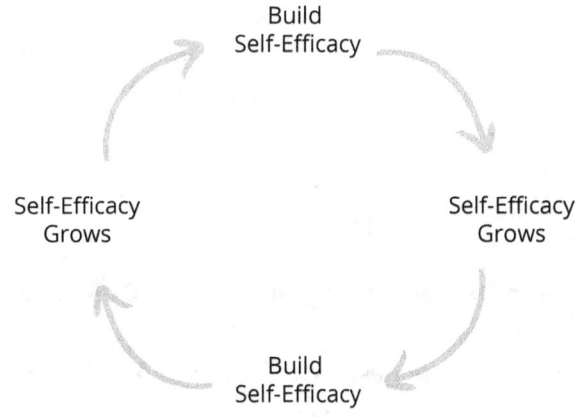

Figure 13: The Cycle of Self-Efficacy

Building Self-Efficacy for Wellbeing

If building self-efficacy grows self-efficacy, we need to know how to proactively build self-efficacy as we work on wellbeing. While there are many ways to build self-efficacy, we also need to focus on those that will improve wellbeing. Let's take a look at those now.

Do Hard Things and Stretch Your Comfort Zone

Bandura says there is no better way to increase self-efficacy than to set a goal, overcome obstacles and work with grit and perseverance to accomplish something, and that by doing this multiple times you will come to believe in your ability to succeed (Moore 2016).

The more we work on our wellbeing, despite how challenging it may be, the more we increase our ability to build self-efficacy and succeed. I know some aspects of teacher wellbeing, and the things you would like to do, either for everyday or workplace wellbeing, may be hard, but the more you work on them, the more the cycle of self-efficacy comes into play.

Whether you choose to work on going to bed earlier or reviewing and changing your assessment cycle to make it more efficient and save time, there will be obstacles and challenges. It is through perseverance, grit, determination and overcoming challenges, such as putting your phone down or letting go of completing more and more assessments, that will allow your self-efficacy to grow.

Find People who Demonstrate your Desired Outcome

People who have what we desire can be huge contributors to our own self-efficacy. Other people's successes allow us to believe that things we may think or feel are out of reach are actually possible. Sometimes, all it takes is finding one person who is doing what you think can't be done to give you the inspiration you need.

A great example of this is Roger Bannister – the first person to run a mile in less than four minutes. He did what everyone thought was humanly impossible, leaving some people shocked, but others inspired. Not long after Bannister achieved the four-minute mile, more and more people started to do so. It was a simple case of, 'Well, if he can do it, so can I' – and from here their self-efficacy increased.

Whatever it is you are setting your sights on, find others who are already doing it. Find the teacher who has mastered their wellbeing or who manages to not take work home or work on weekends, and ask them how to do it and what can you do to achieve it, too. Find the school that has managed to make the curriculum workable, uses meeting time effectively or has highly engaged staff, and again, use this as evidence that it can be done. Learn from them, be curious, and ask questions so you can make these changes too.

Break Things Down into Small Chunks

We can often overthink what needs to be done and create a sense of overwhelm before we even begin. This can contribute to low self-efficacy as we start to feel like it's all too much and it can't be done. To overcome this, we have to break things down into small, achievable chunks.

While having a vision and big picture in mind is a great place to start, we need to break it down – just like we do when we turn the curriculum into unit plans, our unit plans into lessons. The smaller the task, the more achievable it seems, the more confidence we have and the higher our self-efficacy is. From here we can begin to more easily tackle the work we need to do.

Think of it like the Pareto principle (80/20 rule) that is commonly used in business, which states that 80% of our results come from 20% of our effort. If we break down the habits we are trying to build, goals we are trying to achieve or things we are trying to change into 20% chunks, we can amplify the impact much quicker than if we focus on it all at once.

Seek Positive Feedback and Celebrate

The better we feel, the more we want to keep doing what we're doing. We're wired to continuously seek out endorphins (the brain's feel-good chemicals). Seeking positive feedback and celebrating successes will increase self-efficacy.

Seeking positive feedback and celebrating successes also positively impacts our feelings and overall mood. When we are in a more positive state, we naturally feel more confident, can deal with challenges more easily, have more perseverance and are less likely to give up – all which support self-efficacy.

While there may be challenges to overcome or things that are not going the way we would like, more often than not we can find something positive to focus on. One late night to bed out of a whole week does not mean you have failed, and not getting your assessments marked and data entered on time does not mean the new processes you are trying haven't entirely worked. Everything is feedback, and there are always wins, despite the challenges. It is not always easy to see what is working. We are wired with a negative bias, meaning we will more easily see what isn't working than what is. This is okay, as long as you actively spend time seeking positive feedback and celebrating the wins, too.

Now we have looked at self-efficacy, what it is and how it links to skill and will, we will explore collective efficacy and how it supports teacher wellbeing.

What is Collective Efficacy?

As I mentioned in the introduction to Part 3, you may be familiar with the term 'collective teacher efficacy' through your work as a teacher. It featured at number one on John Hattie's meta-analysis of effect size on factors affecting student achievement, with an effect size of 1.57 (Donohoo, Hattie and Eells 2018) and has been the focus of a number of schools and teams for many years now. Collective teacher efficacy is when teachers believe that they and their colleagues can impact student learning (Donohoo 2016). In the space of teaching and learning this is such a powerful and important belief to foster, and, as the research has shown, significantly impacts student outcomes.

Collective teacher efficacy stems from collective efficacy which, again as defined by Bandura (Moore 2016), is a group's shared belief in its ability to organise and execute action and results specific to its ability. Hence, teachers, leaders and those in education working on teacher wellbeing, and more specifically the areas of productivity, engagement and performance and growth, which make up workplace wellbeing, need to share the belief that they can make the changes needed to achieve specific results.

Collective efficacy has contributed to many different groups and teams achieving excellence, not just teachers. It has been evident in sporting teams that foster the belief they can perform better, and in neighbourhoods where the residents believe they can reduce crime and violence or improve health and turn their neighbourhood around. In these examples, all members believed collectively they could make a difference to the problem they were facing. Research shows this is what makes teams and groups more able to persist and overcome challenges (Goddard and Salloum 2012).

Ultimately, we need to build collective efficacy in the colleagues we work with, in our teams, in our schools and across networks and systems. We need to believe we can do the work, have the confidence, know we can make a difference and create impact in this space – and, importantly, that we can do it together. Along with skill, will and self-efficacy, collective efficacy is just as important for workplace wellbeing to thrive. Collective efficacy is the final piece in being able to work on change for teacher wellbeing. If we have all four of these areas then we have people who know what to do, want to do the work needed, believe that they can make a difference, are confident in themselves, and, as a team, have a shared belief that they can make an impact (see table 11).

Skill	Will	Self-Efficacy	Collective Efficacy
'I know how and have the **competence and knowledge**.'	'I want to and I have the **motivation and enthusiasm**.'	'I believe **I can**.'	'I believe **we can**.'

Table 11: Skill, Will, Self-Efficacy and Collective Efficacy

If we know there is a significant benefit from fostering collective teacher efficacy to improve student outcomes, we can harness the power of collective efficacy to bring teachers, leaders and educators together to work on teacher wellbeing.

Building Collective Efficacy for Wellbeing

There are four ways to bring about collective efficacy: mastery experience, vicarious experience, social persuasion and affective states (Bandura 1986 and Goddard et al. 2004, cited in Donohoo 2016).

Mastery experience is when teachers experience and feel successful at something that they have set out to do. The more this happens together, the more collective efficacy and the belief a difference can be made grows – hence teachers are more likely to keep trying new things. If we take, for example, time – which as we have learned is what underpins productivity in workplace wellbeing – and work on ways to reduce time spent on tasks while still achieving the same output, this will make teachers feel successful, increase collective efficacy, and increase motivation to look for and try new ways and approaches. This also has a direct impact on mindset and positive emotion: feelings of success, having more time and knowing that something has worked makes teachers feel like they can achieve the change despite having to overcome obstacles along the way.

To support this, we also need to provide opportunities for staff to have vicarious experiences, meaning they need to see that others have done what they are striving for. This means we need to draw upon the expertise of our colleagues who are doing things the way we want to do them. This could involve teams learning from other teams in a school; or teams and schools visiting, connecting with and seeing the work other educators are doing in the teacher wellbeing space. In education, we tend to do this well for teaching and learning, but not so well for the systems, structures and processes we use to operate.

Schools, while being bound by curriculum, operate differently in just about every way – from planning, to reporting, to assessing, and even how playground duties are designed and allocated. These things that make up our day-to-day operations contribute significantly to teacher wellbeing, yet they can vary significantly. This is one space we can strengthen in order to learn from one another and see how other teams and schools operate. By exploring these areas and allowing for vicarious experience to occur, we can positively influence collective efficacy.

Social persuasion also weighs heavily in building collective efficacy. When groups are encouraged and supported by those they believe to be credible – leaders, or people with significant impact in the area they are trying to succeed in – it can help to build motivation to overcome the lack of confidence and setbacks that impact productivity. Although not as effective on its own, social persuasion is helpful when used with other sources of collective efficacy. While using social persuasion from those within the team or school setting can work, so too can engaging in social persuasion from someone outside of the setting. This can be in the form of talks, workshops, professional development and sharing feedback on achievement (Goddard, Hoy and Hoy, 2004).

Lastly, we have affective states. Although this area is said to have the smallest impact of the four on collective efficacy, it is worth noting that how people or teams feel (their emotional state) can impact their ability to face challenges and persevere. For example, if teachers are feeling overwhelmed with workload or worried about the change that lies ahead, their affective state may be in a place of anxiety or fear. Their confidence and perception of ability may be negatively impacted because of that state, which therefore impacts the team's collective efficacy. If this occurs, it is likely that a team's perception of and willingness to tackle an obstacle may be less effective.

Overall, these four sources of collective efficacy should be considered when establishing and working in teams to build teacher wellbeing. Along with these four areas, we can also work on the structural conditions required to enable collective efficacy.

Improving the conditions in which teachers work is said to increase the likelihood that things will turn out as expected (Donohoo 2016). There are conditional structures schools need to put in place to enable collective efficacy to thrive. The conditions are not necessarily related only to the work of building collective efficacy, but also to the culture of the school. Let's take a look at them now.

Focus on Workplace Wellbeing for Improved Teaching and Learning

There is a belief that teacher wellbeing sits outside of teaching and learning, with schools struggling to know how to prioritise both. What is needed, however, is an understanding that teaching and learning, and the systems, structures and processes around it, are in fact part of teacher wellbeing. When looking at the Teacher Wellbeing Framework for Everyday and Workplace Wellbeing I shared in Chapter 1, you can see this is what is defined as workplace wellbeing, and includes engagement, productivity and performance and growth. If we can understand that this is part of teacher wellbeing, we can influence the collective efficacy of teams and have them more invested in the organisational structures of their school.

With workload having a significant impact on teacher wellbeing, focusing on these areas, as well as the four aspects of collective efficacy, allows for the importance of *how* we do things (through workplace wellbeing) to influence how we feel. By working with school staff to identify key areas of teaching and learning that are impacting teacher wellbeing, and narrowing down what is and isn't in our control, we can select relevant and appropriate areas to focus on. This supports teachers to see the connection, while building their autonomy and influencing collective efficacy.

Establish Clear and Shared Goals

Through establishing clear goals and focusing on areas of workplace wellbeing, we can build collective efficacy in teams. Clear and shared goals help teachers to know what they are expected to be focusing on and gives them permission to put down other things that aren't supporting the main area of focus at this point in time. In most schools, the area of need is often quite extensive. By working through a process to identify clear and shared goals, schools and teams can collectively agree on what to focus on, what to give energy to and what to leave or press pause on for now.

By engaging everyone in this process, we can build collective efficacy through giving teachers autonomy over what is important and most critical right now. When we give teachers autonomy over decision-making and goal setting in this area, we increase their motivation, willingness and confidence that they can achieve what is needed – hence positively impacting collective efficacy.

Build Cohesion and Support Collaboration

Cohesion and collaboration are key to building collective efficacy. Team cohesion refers to how close members of a team feel, how united they are in terms of achieving shared goals, and having everyone work together despite other factors. Strong team cohesion can also increase social persuasion.

When teams are cohesive, collaboration is more effective, with some saying you cannot have collaboration without cohesion. For the sake of teacher wellbeing, I have to agree with this. If we want to build strong collective efficacy and have teams that fundamentally believe the work they do can make a difference to individual and collective wellbeing, we have to promote and work to build cohesiveness and collaboration in staff and among teams.

Failure to build cohesion and collaboration will result in individual teachers or teams working on what they feel is best, but without alignment to a whole-school vision, and without consistency across staff. This can in return impact collective efficacy as teachers and teams work with competing agendas. Therefore, cohesion and collaboration are needed to improve workplace wellbeing, teaching and learning. Without people interacting and working together, collective efficacy will drop.

Invest, Review and Celebrate

While you're building and maintaining collective efficacy you must prioritise the investment being made, review what is or isn't working and celebrate along the way. It can be easy to focus on the task at hand as opposed to the people who are making it happen. Part of maintaining collective efficacy, be it in the space of teacher wellbeing or anywhere else, is recognising that it is a case of people before performance.

If we lose sight of the people – our teachers, who are the drivers of the work – their confidence, belief and perseverance can be damaged due to not feeling supported or valued. We have to make sure we invest in our teachers carrying out this work, be it through time, guidance, professional development or resources. We need to make these a priority. Failure to do this instantly provides an obstacle that doesn't need to be there. Regularly reviewing and celebrating also puts people ahead of performance. Through doing this we shine a light on what is going well, address obstacles and offer support, and build confidence and motivation through acknowledging success – all of which continually support collective efficacy.

Collective efficacy is perhaps not as simple as self-efficacy in that it requires the work of multiple teachers and school staff, and also requires support from leadership and decision-makers to allow the time, energy and money needed to prioritise teacher wellbeing. However, if we begin with both the four sources needed for collective efficacy and the four areas to build collective efficacy to support teacher wellbeing, we are off to a great start. From here these things will grow and become embedded in our approach to supporting teacher wellbeing – which, in theory, is what all teachers and schools should be aiming to do if we are to move away from the one-off, band-aid approaches we have, up until now, been relying on.

Chapter Summary

- We need both self-efficacy and collective efficacy to support teacher wellbeing in schools.
- Self-efficacy is the belief and confidence of an individual; collective efficacy is the belief and confidence of a team.
- Skill and will help to ensure we have the knowledge, skills and motivation needed to make change.
- When we have high self and collective efficacy, our ability to persist, have confidence and work through challenges is much greater than when we have low self and collective efficacy.
- There are four sources needed to bring about collective efficacy: mastery experience, vicarious experiences, social persuasion and affective states.

From Theory to Action

Let's look at some reflection questions for each area that will help you to build self-efficacy, the four sources for collective efficacy, and collective efficacy.

Building Self-Efficacy	
1. Do hard things and stretch your comfort zone	• What do you know you should be doing that you have been putting off because it is uncomfortable? • What would one step outside of your comfort zone look like? • How would you feel if you took this step?
2. Find people who demonstrate your desired outcome	• Who do you know who has what you are striving for? • What are they doing that you could learn from? • What else do you need to find out from them? What questions could you ask them?
3. Break things down into small chunks	• With your big goal in mind, what are the small chunks you could break this into? • What would it look like if you were halfway towards your goal? One quarter? One eighth? • How can you use this to help you break it down into small chunks?
4. Seek positive feedback and celebrate	• What is going well? • What do you need to celebrate? • What stops you from celebrating?

Building Self-Efficacy – The Four Sources	
1. Mastery experience	• What evidence do you have that what you are aiming for is possible? • Have you or someone you know already achieved this? • Can you find multiple examples of success in this area?
2. Vicarious experience	• Who or what school is achieving what you are aiming for? • How can you connect with and learn from them? • What questions could you ask them?

Building Self-Efficacy – The Four Sources

3.	Social persuasion	• What professional development could support you? • Who do you know that could offer guidance or support? • With the challenges you face, are there any experts or knowledgeable people you know who you could draw upon?
4.	Affective states	• What feelings do you have regarding this work? • Are there any negative states that may impact your ability to work on this? • How could you overcome this and/or increase positive states as you embark on this work?

Building Collective Efficacy for Teacher Wellbeing

1.	Focus on workplace wellbeing for improved teaching and learning	• What areas of teaching and learning are impacting your wellbeing right now? • What is in your control and out of your control? • What one area would be easiest to focus on and have a significant impact on your wellbeing?
2.	Establish clear and shared goals	• What are the shared goals of the team? • Which do you agree is the most important? • Are the goals as clear and precise as possible, and is there a shared understanding of what they mean and the desired result?
3.	Build cohesion and support collaboration	• Are staff aware of the difference between cohesive and collaborative teams? Do they know the characteristics of each? • How can you build more cohesion in your teams? • How can you build more collaboration in your teams?
4.	Invest, review and celebrate	• How does your school invest in the work needed to support teacher wellbeing? • What processes are in place to review the work being done? • How are success and achievements celebrated?

Chapter 8

What can I do? Practical Strategies for Teachers

*When we work from a place, I believe, that says 'I'm enough,'
then we stop screaming and start listening,
we're kinder and gentler to the people around us,
and we're kinder and gentler to ourselves.*
– Brené Brown

With all the theory and research that exists to support aspects of wellbeing, there are proven actions teachers can take to work on their own wellbeing. The strategies we looked at in Part 2 – energy and function, resilience and emotional regulation – are key, but so too is adopting everyday ways of being, behaviours and actions that support all areas of wellbeing.

Most teachers by now have mastered their understanding of self-care, and know that they need to rest, make time for themselves and do things that make them feel good. However, despite teachers knowing this, there are many struggling to put this into action – whether consistently or at all.

Many teachers have the mindset 'I can wait until the weekend' or 'I'll be fine, holidays are soon'. We are also too heavily relying on the aspect of doing something (self-care) to change our overall wellbeing. From what you have read so far, I am sure you can see this is not enough, and that there is so much more to be done.

While self-care most definitely does matter, there are bigger, more transferable skills and actions that teachers need to develop to make their wellbeing a priority. As the components of everyday wellbeing are connected to both subjective and psychological wellbeing, what we need are strategies that support all areas of wellbeing so they become part of our everyday life.

Along with strategies, we also need to continually check back in with how we want to feel and be. You may recall from the introduction when I shared my own story that this was a key turning point for me: focusing on how I wanted to feel and be, before focusing on what to do. It is knowing how you want to feel, and who you want to be, that will help you to figure out what you want or need to do. For example, if you want to feel more energised during the day and be someone who is more present with their family, you may want to adjust some things that impact your energy and function; or if you want to feel calm and less rushed during the day, you may want to be someone who is more organised, which means developing some systems and strategies to help with getting ahead so you can be prepared for the day or week in advance.

Using the formula in figure 14, take a minute to reflect on how you want to feel and be, and use this to identify what it is you may want or need to do.

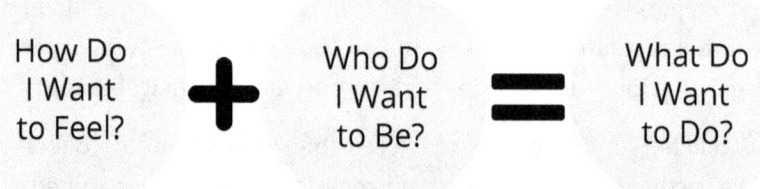

Figure 14: The Feel, Be, Do Formula

Through my own trial and error, study, research and working with others, I have learned there are a number of contributing factors that help teachers prioritise wellbeing, and make this a part of who they are, not just what they do. The five factors worth mastering that contribute to teacher wellbeing are listed in figure 15.

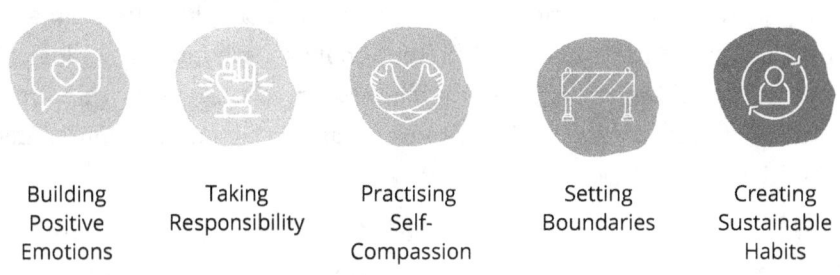

Figure 15: Contributing Factors to Successful Teacher Wellbeing

If you are going to work on your wellbeing, choosing an area to focus on from everyday or workplace wellbeing is a start – but you then have to identify which other strategies are needed to make this happen.

Building Positive Emotions

Building positive emotions is something I have become better at over the years, and I have come to realise it is necessary to my own wellbeing. As with working on understanding emotions and choosing how we respond or react, building positive emotions is a skill we can develop resources around.

As previously discussed, the idea of 'just thinking happy thoughts' or 'snapping out of it and being happy' is not a healthy way to build positive emotions. We have already identified these phrases as examples of toxic positivity. To build positive emotions in a healthy way, so they contribute to our wellbeing, I suggest using a theory developed by Barbra Fredrickson known as the broaden-and-build theory of positive emotions.

The broaden-and-build theory supports the idea that positive emotions are an essential component of optimal functioning and overall wellbeing. It suggests that negative emotions limit our thought-action repertoire – the impact our emotions have on our action – whereas positive emotions expand our thought-action repertoire, allowing us to be more creative, curious, playful and experimental (Celestine 2016). The theory also suggests that positive emotions help to broaden people's attention and thinking, undo lingering negative emotional arousal, fuel psychological resilience, build consequential personal resources, trigger upward spirals towards greater wellbeing in the future, and seed human flourishing (Fredrickson 2004).

From this we can see the importance of cultivating positive emotions in our everyday lives, and that when we do this, we are impacting more than just that specific moment. Through seeking out positive emotions and engaging in activities that build and evoke positive emotions, we can reap the benefits of doing so and influence multiple areas of our lives, including at work. By engaging more frequently in activities that boost positive emotions, we are able to think more clearly and focus for longer, which helps with productivity, engagement and performance and growth, reduces negative thoughts, allows us to be more resilient when facing challenges and positively impacts those around us, including colleagues and students.

It is important to focus on and actively seek out positive emotions, not only because of the benefits I've mentioned, but also because as humans we naturally experience fewer positive emotions than negative emotions on a day-to-day basis. As we naturally have a negative bias, it is common for us to focus on the negative aspects of a situation, including the problem, obstacle or issue, and not acknowledge the positive aspects despite there being perhaps just as many. Our emotional vocabulary is more extensive when it comes to describing negative emotions than positive emotions. As a result of this, we have to actively seek out experiences to build positive emotions each and every day.

There are no suggested or correct ways to build positive emotions; rather, it is suggested we find ways to experience more joy, contentment, love and interest (Fredrickson 1998). This could be done in many ways.

Professionally speaking, you could identify and celebrate things that have worked well that day or things you have achieved; you could spend time with your team because your relationships are positive and always bring about joy; or you could finish that to-do list and feel a sense of achievement and excitement for what you can do next. Table 12 shows other words you may use to describe these emotions and the thought-action response they create. I encourage you to spend some time reflecting on each of these emotions and asking how you could cultivate more experiences to bring these about each day.

Joy	Love
Amusement	Made up of joy, contentment
Exhilaration	and interest
Elation	(ignites the need to repeat these
Gladness	desires within safe,
(ignites the desire to play)	close relationships)
Contentment	**Interest**
Tranquillity	Curiosity
Serenity	Intrigue
(ignites the savour and integrate)	Wonder
	Excitement
	(ignites the desire to explore)

Table 12: Expansion of the Sub-Set of Four Emotions and Thought-Action Repertoire
(Source: Adapted from Fredrickson 1998 and 2004)

Rather than waiting until the weekend, holidays or some designated self-care time, the idea is we find more ways to seek out the positive emotions in table 12 more often. This may mean choosing an experience each day and building these into your routine – be it at home or in the classroom, or looking for different ways to bring about positive emotions. The more you do this, the easier it becomes, and the more you will look for ways to continue the positive cycle. Positive emotions are addictive. We like to feel good, so the more we are able to experience positive emotions, the more frequently we will seek them out.

When I set about on my own journey to cultivate more positive emotions, I became quite good at identifying things that did or did not bring them about. For some things, like housework or paying bills, I also had to recognise that the initial moment of beginning these tasks may not put me in a positive state, but the end result most certainly did. Unlike self-care, some things we can do to build positive emotions might be perceived as being a challenge or even annoying to do in the moment, but they're worth it in the end. Exercise is a great example. It can be hard to get started and challenging during it, but the endorphins we receive afterwards certainly increase our positive emotions, making us want to do it again.

Taking Responsibility

I want to start this section by saying that taking responsibility is not about putting the issue of teacher wellbeing back onto our teachers to solve themselves. We know that there are systemic issues that have been around for a long time that we cannot change, but that we are fighting for and not giving up on. What I mean by taking responsibility is that we need to be aware of and focus on what we *can* control, and exercise responsibility for this.

Based on my own experiences, and those of schools and teachers I have worked with and learned from, there are a number of things both in and out of our control that impact our everyday and workplace wellbeing. This also relates to the locus of control theory we looked at in Chapter 7.

Knowing what is and isn't in our control as teachers can support us to know where we should spend our time and energy and what to focus on for our wellbeing to improve. In my experience, there are always similarities and differences from teacher to teacher, team to team and school to school. Please take this into account as you read the items in figure 16 and know that there will be some variables and differences depending on your circumstances, experiences and environment. There may also be some things that you feel should cross both areas; this is okay too. I have also placed some things across both areas – for example, how we spend our time, which is sometimes both in and out of our control.

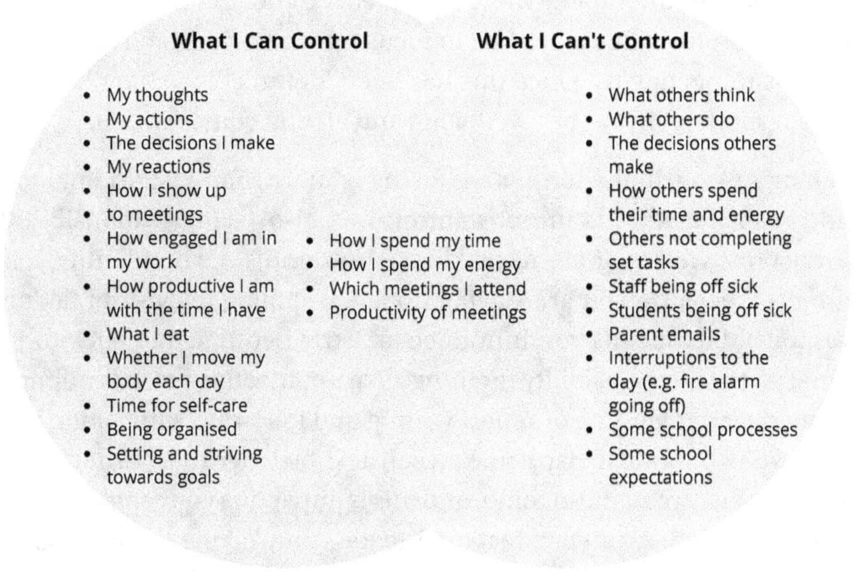

What I Can Control

- My thoughts
- My actions
- The decisions I make
- My reactions
- How I show up
- to meetings
- How engaged I am in my work
- How productive I am with the time I have
- What I eat
- Whether I move my body each day
- Time for self-care
- Being organised
- Setting and striving towards goals

- How I spend my time
- How I spend my energy
- Which meetings I attend
- Productivity of meetings

What I Can't Control

- What others think
- What others do
- The decisions others make
- How others spend their time and energy
- Others not completing set tasks
- Staff being off sick
- Students being off sick
- Parent emails
- Interruptions to the day (e.g. fire alarm going off)
- Some school processes
- Some school expectations

Figure 16: Teacher Wellbeing Influences: Examples of What I Can and Can't Control

The responsibility we need to take for our own wellbeing centres around what we can control. While we can't control some things to do with teaching, such as what others do or think, the amount of parent emails we receive or perhaps some school expectations, it doesn't mean we don't care – and if the issue is impacting teacher wellbeing, it should be addressed. However, in the space of individual responsibility and to look at practical strategies individual teachers can apply for their own wellbeing, I encourage you in this instance to focus on what you *can* control.

When I went through a period of burnout and experienced chronic stress, looking back I can see I was giving a lot of time and energy to things I couldn't control. This caused me to become fixated on areas that I couldn't do anything about. Because I didn't fully understand this, the time, effort and energy I was putting in was, among other things, partly to blame for the burnout I experienced.

It is important we identify and know what we can and can't control in regard to what impacts our own wellbeing (to figure this out for yourself, please complete the 'From Theory to Action' tasks at the end of this chapter). This allows us to focus on what we can change, and what is impacting us. Once this has been identified, we then have to take responsibility for our wellbeing and all that comes with it.

Taking responsibility for our wellbeing is more than just acceptance and realising what is in our control; it is also taking responsibility for actions we are or are not taking. For example, if you identify you are tired because you are staying up late watching television, taking responsibility means you introduce an early bedtime and stick to it. You can take responsibility for things like not meeting work deadlines around team planning or report writing and follow up with actions so it doesn't continue to happen. You can acknowledge that perhaps you are in a negative frame of mind, and this is impacting your engagement and contribution to your teaching team – but taking responsibility means you are also actively working to change these things.

Taking responsibility means three things – acknowledgement, action and behaviour change.

Practising Self-Compassion

Self-compassion means treating yourself the same way you would treat others, especially those who are experiencing challenges or overcoming obstacles. Understanding how this is a part of wellbeing means acknowledging that the journey of wellbeing, the change we may need to go though, the obstacles, setbacks and difficulties to overcome are part of the shared journey through wellbeing. The more compassion you can give to yourself, the easier this will become.

We are often our own worst critics and give ourselves the hardest time. We tend to hold ourselves to the highest expectations, put the most pressure on ourselves and are the least forgiving when it comes to things we feel we haven't done right. These traits are not self-compassion and get in the way of our ability to act with kindness when it comes to working on our own wellbeing.

When it comes to working on our everyday or workplace wellbeing, we will undoubtedly find things out about ourselves that perhaps we do not like, or that we wish we had already changed. It could be recognising that we don't move our body or exercise as much as we want, that we don't have the skills needed to regulate our emotions and we constantly feel like we could break down any minute, or maybe that our resilience strategies are more to the maladaptive side or we need to be finding more positive ways release stress. When we look at our workplace wellbeing, we may find that we are not as productive as we could be, or our engagement is down because we've been focusing on things we can't control instead of what we can control, or that even though we want to commit to a goal of improving how we teach we just don't have the energy to do so. No matter what we discover, we have to execute a level of self-compassion. It's self-compassion that will allow us to continue to grow and move forward to work on our wellbeing. Self-compassion also helps us to realise that we've all been doing the best we can with what we've got, and that is good enough.

The truth is, everyone has been doing the best they can with what they've got up until this point. Be it a teacher, a school leader or someone who's making the decisions, we're all just trying to do the best we can. It's because of this we need self-compassion if we're going to be able to move forward and beyond the current space in which we are. We can talk about things like taking responsibility, building habits or setting boundaries, but no matter what it is we're trying to do, we have to be compassionate to ourselves. We have to be compassionate, show ourselves kindness and understanding, and build back the trust we need within ourselves to be able to make change. When we bring in self-compassion, we enhance our self-efficacy and together these two things will help to improve our everyday and workplace wellbeing.

Dr Kristin Neff (2022), an expert in self-compassion, has identified three components that are needed to build self-compassion: self-kindness, humanity and mindfulness (see table 13 overleaf).

Self-kindness	Self-kindness means you identify that all people, including you, experience setbacks or obstacles, and that this does not make you a failure, impact your self-worth, or mean you can't improve. Self-kindness does not judge and allows people to be gentle with themselves.
Humanity	Self-compassion with humanity means you understand that all humans suffer and it is not exclusive to you. Humanity allows you to recognise others around you may also be experiencing what you are and to give yourself the same compassion as you would them.
Mindfulness	Self-compassion also requires similar work to that of emotional regulation, in that we recognise that no emotions or feelings need to be overlooked or amplified. Mindfulness allows us to be present in the space, to observe thoughts and feelings as they come, and to be non-judgemental and more compassionate.

Table 13: Neff's Three Components of Self-Compassion
(Source: Adapted from Neff 2022)

These three areas can help to build teacher wellbeing through supporting teachers to see that while they may be feeling they have failed with their wellbeing, that isn't actually true. No teacher has failed. All anyone has done is the best they can, and sometimes that meant choosing students, work, or burning out before realising something needed to shift. No matter where any teacher is in their journey of wellbeing, self-compassion is needed.

When you reflect on your own wellbeing journey, be it everyday or workplace wellbeing, act with compassion. Give yourself the kindness you need without judgement; act with humanity and know you are not alone or in isolation; and be mindful in your approach, recognising how you feel but not attaching to the emotion or feeling. With true self-compassion you can recognise things for what they are, let them go and move forward.

Setting Boundaries

Boundaries, as defined by Brené Brown (2015), are 'our list of what's okay and what's not okay'. Boundaries can also be thought of as what you allow into your world, what you accept, what makes you happy, or your rules for your life. Boundaries are often connected to our beliefs and values and act as the gatekeeper for how we want to live. For teacher wellbeing, boundaries can be broken into two areas: workplace boundaries and personal boundaries. While there may be some overlap, there may also be some key differences to the boundaries you set for your professional and personal life.

Some of us already know and are comfortable acting in line with our boundaries, but this might be a new area of work to do for others. Regardless of whether you are new or old to setting boundaries, it's work that is worth doing. People who set boundaries are said to have good mental and emotional health, more autonomy over their life and a better sense of identity, whereas those who lack boundaries are said to experience more resentment, anger and burnout (Selva 2018).

Boundaries exist to help us live life to a standard we seek; however, while we get to decide our own personal and workplace boundaries, in some cases they may also impact others. Boundaries around behaviours, actions or language being used – such as saying no when you can't take on anything else, not having your emails on your phone or not taking work home – are all boundaries you can choose to have, but at the same time you need to be mindful of how these may impact others.

A few years into my teaching career, I made a conscious effort to not do so much work out of the school environment, and to put some boundaries in place to create space between my work and home life. One of these boundaries was not having my emails on my phone, and not checking them once I had left work. One morning I arrived at school at around 7:45 am and, as I entered the school building, a leader asked me what I thought of a particular email that had been sent. I shared with them I had not read it yet as I hadn't yet checked my emails. This reply was not taken well, and a response was made saying I needed to make more time to check emails. My commitment to my work was also questioned because I shared I didn't have work emails on my personal phone. At this moment I was quite taken aback by this comment, as I had left work at 5 pm the evening before, and I had only just arrived back the following morning.

When I reflected on this event – which to be honest did shock me and cause me to have an emotional reaction that I needed to manage before I responded – what I realised was that while I had put in place a boundary not to check emails outside of school time, I hadn't communicated this to anyone. Communication is a key part of boundary setting if your boundary impacts others. Moving forward from this event, I made a conscious effort to inform those who needed to know that I did not have emails on my phone and I did not check them outside work hours; however, if there was an emergency then please call me. Often colleagues were accepting of this, however every now and then someone would react in a way that let me know they didn't agree. Coming back to what we can and can't control, we can't control what others might think of our boundaries, but we can control what boundaries we set, how we communicate them and how we go about enacting them.

We have to be aware that while we have boundaries in certain areas, others may either disagree or not share the same boundary. We are not responsible for other people's boundaries and what they deem to be acceptable or not; however, we are responsible for our own boundaries and ensuring that they are adhered to.

When setting boundaries there are three steps I encourage you to take:
1. *Identify and define.* Know what your boundary is, be clear and concise, and be confident with the boundary you have put in place.
2. *Communicate with others.* Communication is key to having successful boundaries. You need to communicate boundaries to others in your life, especially if it impacts them or if they have crossed your boundary.
3. *Be prepared to say no.* Whether your boundaries are personal or professional saying no to things will be key to upholding them. Not everyone is comfortable with saying no or hearing no, so it might be a good idea to practise what you would say and have a few key phrases to draw upon if needed.

Creating Sustainable Habits

Habits, like wellbeing, is somewhat of a buzzword and trendy thing to do. In saying that, though, developing purposeful habits is important. It takes something that you simply do, and makes it part of who you are. Our habits also influence and shape our identity. As Jack Canfield, author of *The Success Principles*, says, 'Your habits will determine your future'. If that is true, it makes sense to build good habits, and many of them.

Habits can either be conscious or unconscious; either way, they still impact how you feel and behave. For example, you may have a conscious habit of tidying your desk every afternoon before you go home, which makes you feel calm the next morning when you arrive. You may have a conscious habit of organising your outfit the night before to save time in the morning. Or you may have an unconscious habit of eating chocolate after dinner each night, or of sitting on the lounge each afternoon and playing on your phone for 30 minutes or more.

I approach building habits for teacher wellbeing using my HABITS acronym:

H: Honour where you are.
A: Ask yourself: 'How do I want to feel?' and 'Who do I want to be?'
B: Build a plan – what do you need to do?
I: Implement each step.
T: Take your time.
S: Surrender to what is.

Let's take a closer look at each of these six steps.

H: Honour Where You Are

This is the act of bringing self-compassion into change. Before you begin, you must honour and accept where you are without judgement. At times change can come because we are unhappy, frustrated or have had enough of our current situation. Feeling this is enough. Honouring where you are means accepting this for what it is and not falling into a cycle of blame, justification or judgement.

If we don't honour where we are, and instead put blame or judgement on ourselves, we may find ourselves thinking things such as 'I am not good enough', 'I should have done better by now' or 'I am a failure'. This way of thinking only increases negative emotions, which we know then make it more difficult to think openly, creatively or with curiosity – all of which are needed when building habits.

Up until this point, you have been doing the best you can. Acknowledge that. Use this moment to celebrate all the amazing things you have done and who you are. Don't rush and feel as if you need to push past this place quickly – while it might be the catalyst for change, you need to be kind to yourself.

A: Ask Yourself: 'How Do I Want to Feel?' and 'Who Do I Want to Be?'

When we seek to build habits, we often just go straight to what we are going to change or do. Instead, we need to take some time to ask ourselves who we want to be, and how we want to feel. Our habits aren't just what we do, they are us.

So, who do you want to be? This may mean coming back to your values and deciding you want to be healthy, kind, productive, resourceful, determined, successful or peaceful. The options for who you can be are endless, but you need to develop the habits that support that.

Then, how do you want to feel? Do you want to feel more energised, calm, organised, content, connected to your team, present in your class or on top of all your work tasks? Again, the options are endless, so take the time needed to figure out how you want to feel.

After this, choose some keywords that resonate with you, and that you know would help in multiple areas of your life. For example, you may want to be and feel healthy, so for that you are going to build habits around the five areas in energy and function; or you may want to be and feel more calm, so you are going to work on building habits to support your emotional regulation strategies.

B: Build a Plan – What Do You Need to Do?

Now you have accepted where you are, and how you want to feel and know who you want to be, you can begin to build a plan (notice that this is not step one). This is where you may like to write a goal to help begin the habit. It is also important to break the habit you want to build into small steps.

Firstly, start with the end in mind. What would this look like? How would you feel? Break this into small, achievable steps. For example, if you want to start a new habit of moving your body each morning, starting with seven days a week may be too much of a change, so instead aim for two or three mornings a week. Once you have built this habit you can increase it.

Another thing to consider are the systems you may need to implement alongside building the habit. In his book *Atomic Habits*, James Clear (2018) states, 'You do not rise to the level of your goals. You fall to the level of your systems.' This means the systems you put in place matter as much as the goal. It is not enough to say you want to move your body each morning; you need to think about what you need to do to make that happen. Do you need to place your workout clothes by your bed the night before? Do you need to tell the people in your household so they know what you are doing (also great for accountability)? Or do you need to go to bed and get up earlier? The systems you implement make the goal happen, and once your goal consistently happens, it becomes a habit.

I: Implement Each Step

Once you have broken your goals down into small, achievable steps, you can begin to implement them. If you are wanting to leave work at work, you might need to overhaul how you use your time during the day, create new systems for planning or marking or try other new ways of doing things. But all of this takes time. So, instead of starting by drawing a line in the sand and declaring you will no longer be taking work home, which winds up causing you more stress and overwhelm because you haven't developed the system to support that, just choose one night a week to do it. This is step one.

By breaking your plan down into small, achievable steps it will help you to easily achieve success without feeling overwhelmed or resistant because the change is too big, or you don't have the systems you need to support the habit. Building habits happens one step at a time.

T: Take Your Time

You need to take your time. Another downfall when we try to instil new habits is we don't give them the time they need to become habits. When we first start creating a habit, it requires time and energy to create a new way of being and doing. This can be challenging and difficult. Starting a new habit also requires a lot more thinking than continuing a habit you have already formed.

Activities like cleaning your teeth, getting dressed and even driving to school are all well-ingrained habits that don't require much energy. You can do them on autopilot. You don't need to think through each step or ask yourself 'What's next?', you just do it. Once we complete a task over and over, it becomes a habit, and requires less time, energy and conscious thought. This is how you know you have developed a habit. Expecting yourself to take on a new habit instantly is a recipe for disappointment.

S: Surrender to What Is

Lastly, when creating a new habit, you may need to, at times, surrender to what is. Things are going to get in the way of the habit you are trying to create, and sometimes you can't do much about it. Say you are building the habit of eating more nutritious foods, but you accidently leave your lunch at home and have to choose from the limited options at the canteen; or you are building a habit of not taking work home, and then realise that isn't possible when you have to write reports, or the week you are on school camp. Things will happen. The important part is to surrender to them and not let them get in the way of coming back to the habit you are building.

Just as we looked at what we can and can't control in the section on taking responsibility earlier in this chapter, there will be things you can't control that get in the way of the habit you are trying to create. What you can control however are your thoughts around it, the decisions you make, and how you respond to it. (From personal experience I can tell you that stressing about it or being annoyed really doesn't help.) Getting back to the habit as soon as possible is what matters. This is the art of surrendering to what is.

The five strategies we've covered in this chapter are designed to support whatever area of wellbeing you are working on. Whether you are focusing on your everyday or workplace wellbeing (or both), these strategies are applicable to all areas. The more you master these, the more your wellbeing will flourish.

Chapter Summary

- Along with areas of wellbeing to develop, there are underpinning strategies that are needed to put these into action.
- There are five key strategies to work on for everyday and workplace wellbeing: building positive emotions, taking responsibility, practising self-compassion, setting boundaries and creating sustainable habits.
- When creating a new habit use the HABITS acronym.
- As you implement these strategies it is important to give them time to integrate into your daily life.
- Everyone's journey will be different, meaning we need to act without judgement for ourselves and others as we make changes.

From Theory to Action

Let's look at some practical ways to work on each of the five key strategies to help build your everyday and workplace wellbeing.

1.	Building positive emotions	Find ways to build more joy, contentment, interest and love in your everyday life. For example, watch something funny, draw upon happy memories, practise meditation, keep a gratitude journal, spend time with friends and family, exercise, spend time in nature or engage in some self-care.
2.	Taking responsibility	Follow these steps to help figure out what you need to take responsibility for: • What is impacting your wellbeing right now? List each item on a separate piece of paper or Post-it. • Sort the notes into two categories: things you can control and things you can't control. • Looking at the 'things you can control' notes, choose what you are going to begin to take responsibility for. • Note down some actions you are going to take. • Draw upon strategies for boundary setting and building habits.
3.	Practising self-compassion	Notice where you are judging yourself, being negative towards yourself, or feeling shame or guilt. Ask yourself the following questions: • How could you be more self-compassionate? • How could you practise self-kindness? • What would you say or do to someone else in the same situation? How can you apply this to yourself?
4.	Setting boundaries	Work through the three steps of setting boundaries in both your personal and professional life: • identify and define • communicate with others • be prepared to say no.
5.	Creating sustainable habits	Choose an area of everyday or workplace wellbeing you would like to build a habit around and begin to work through the HABITS acronym.

Chapter 9

What can we do? Practical Strategies for Schools

The most meaningful way to succeed is to help others succeed.
– Adam Grant

Note: in this chapter I will use the term 'school,' however this can also mean leadership team, pre-school, kindergarten or early learning centre, school leaders, wellbeing team or whomever in your school is responsible for making the decisions in this space.

The question of what schools can do for teacher wellbeing is one that is often asked by schools themselves. What can we do? What are we responsible for? How can we do this on top of everything else? This chapter will help answer these important questions.

Schools can do a number of things to support teacher wellbeing, but first, having an understanding of what teacher wellbeing is, the difference between everyday and workplace wellbeing, and what this looks like in your school is going to be important. We know that wellbeing, including teacher wellbeing, is a complex issue that is not universally defined; therefore, as a school you need to know what teacher wellbeing means for you, before you decide what to do about it (if you're unsure, head back to Part 1 to recap).

What each school does about teacher wellbeing needs to be contextualised to their school. There is no one-size-fits-all approach to how a school manages or improves teacher wellbeing, and there shouldn't be. Every school operates differently, is organised differently, has different staff and different priorities, and this needs to be taken into account when building a strategy to work on teacher wellbeing.

In regards to the responsibility a school should have – and I know this is a much-debated topic – I believe schools should work on ensuring teachers feel safe, supported and have the resources needed to do their job well. Schools should also ensure their teachers are provided opportunities to learn about everyday wellbeing and how they can improve this, as well as work together to look at aspects of workplace wellbeing and actively seek out ways to make these things a priority. This means too that schools should aim to have the systems, structures and processes in place to support teachers' everyday and workplace wellbeing.

For this to happen easily and effectively, there are five factors for schools to consider which contribute significantly to enhancing teacher wellbeing (see figure 17).

Building Positive Relationships | Setting a Clear Vision with Supportive Goals | Utilising Staff Strengths | Having Strong Infrastructure | Fostering Flexibility

Figure 17: Contributing Factors for Schools to Enhance Teacher Wellbeing

These five strategies will help to build a culture in your school that allows all other areas to develop. If we don't have positive staff relationships, know the long-term vision, work to our strengths, support our staff through strong infrastructure including systems, structures and processes, and pay attention to impact, we haven't built the foundations for teacher wellbeing to thrive.

Building Positive Relationships

In any work setting, positive or negative relationships among staff influence how staff perform. When staff have positive relationships with their colleagues, this makes them more productive and supportive of one another, and increases psychological safety. Focusing on building positive relationships also influences overall school culture and creates a more encouraging place for staff to work. Relationships are a key feature to improving wellbeing – humans are inherently social creatures and we need to be continually supported, loved and valued by others (Seligman 2012).

Another reason to focus on building positive relationships among staff is that the better our relationships are, the less impacted we may be by stress as we know we have others to support us. Positive relationships also benefit staff as they help to create a positive culture where others are more likely to ask for help, offer support, act with empathy and be more motivated and engaged. Research has also shown that the more positive relationships and opportunities for connection we foster in the workspace, the more we promote trust, respect and confidence, with employees believing in one another and inspiring each other in their performance (Geue 2018). To create this environment, we must provide opportunities for staff to connect socially and professionally, and to get to know each other beyond their job description.

Given the benefits to both everyday and workplace wellbeing and that positive relationships among staff can increase productivity, engagement, performance and growth, schools will benefit from looking for ways to improve staff relationships in the work environment. There are multiple ways to do this. It's worth being intentional about it, by considering and planning for these opportunities in advance as part of school infrastructure – not as an afterthought, or a single end-of-term event. It is also more beneficial to make opportunities for connection face-to-face.

Figure 18 shows some ways schools can increase positive relationships between their staff members:

- *Plan ahead.* Planning ahead for staff connection opportunities means opportunities to do so are scheduled into the term and school year calendar. This could mean building opportunities into staff meeting time, offering different social events throughout the year, or having weekly activities staff can opt to join.
- *Provide time.* Building relationships and connection takes time. If activities are planned outside of regular meetings or work times, people may not be able to attend. This means, as a school, we must make time within our already existing structures for staff to connect. Now I know that some may feel we have too many other pressing things to do, and that often when something else comes along that is deemed more important, these opportunities are often the first to go. However, if the benefits of positive staff connection include things such as increased positive culture and more support for one another, the advantages of sacrificing one meeting time could come back in more ways than one.
- *Find different ways to connect.* Find different ways to connect and get to know each other and build them into how your school operates. This means finding ways to allow people to get to know each other on a personal and professional level. Finding out about a colleague's family, interests, skills or strengths outside of work improves positive relationships. Alongside staff meetings that build on opportunities for connection, you may also like to consider different ways to include connection within regular meetings. For example, adding in staff shoutouts always boosts relationships; and having a 'phone a friend' item on your agenda may allow staff to ask for help in an area that has been bothering them, and give someone else the opportunity to step forward to offer assistance – hence strengthening their relationship and building positivity within the overall team.

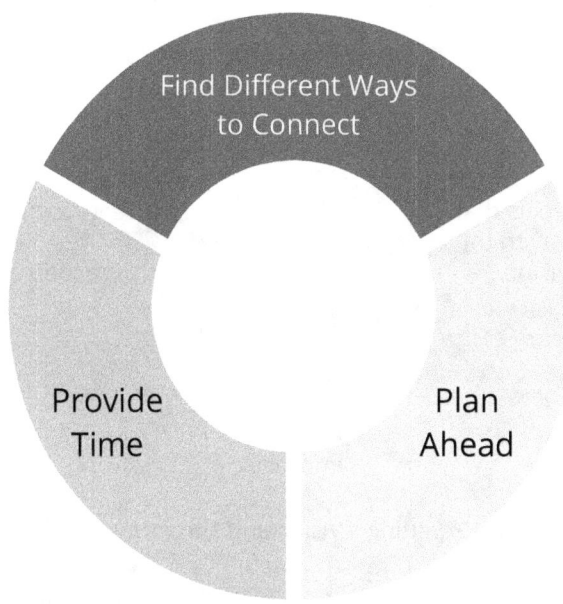

Figure 18: Building Positive Relationships between Staff

Note: having already looked at collective efficacy, and the importance of building cohesive and collaborative teams, I have not included these two strategies here – however they do provide an alternate way to build positive relationships to support teacher wellbeing.

Setting a Clear Vision with Supportive Goals

What is your school's vision for working on teacher wellbeing? How do you want your staff to be, feel, act and think? This is the vision you need to cultivate before working on what to do. There are several steps involved in creating a vision and supportive goals (see figure 19 overleaf).

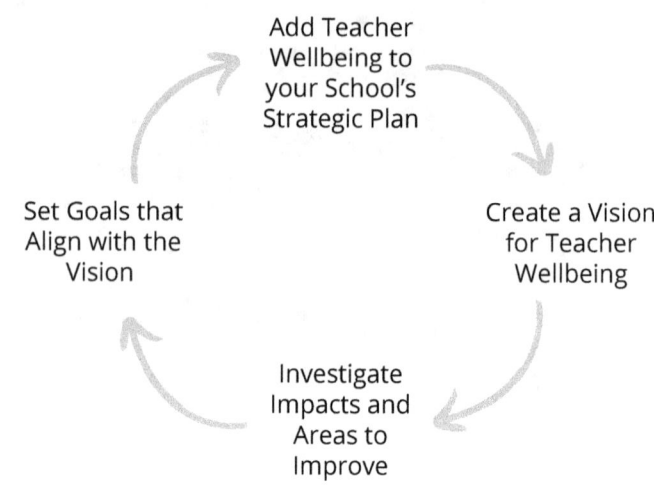

Figure 19: Setting a Vision and Supportive Goals

As this is a vision for teacher wellbeing at your school, it is imperative it's created in collaboration with all stakeholders, as they are the ones it will impact. Many teachers will be able to tell you what is affecting their wellbeing, but leaders don't often ask them how they would like to feel and be, what changes they think could realistically be made, and where to start.

A school leader once asked me if it was worth asking staff what was impacting their wellbeing, or if it was better to just start making changes. If we don't ask our staff, including teachers, what is impacting their wellbeing, how do we know we are making the right changes? We need to consult with our staff, ask questions, seek to understand, and show them we value them and their input before announcing the changes we are making.

We need to consult with staff to find out what they feel would benefit them, what is getting in the way of their wellbeing and what changes they would like made. We need to bring them in to create the vision – our ideal utopia, if you like – and together discuss possible options, strategies and clear objectives.

If we jump straight to trying to fix such a complex issue as teacher wellbeing without finding out what is going on for our staff, we are only going to be able to make changes based on our perception – and our perception, as a principal or a group of leaders and teachers, could be significantly different to what is actually occurring. We need real, relevant data to be able to make real, relevant change.

Once we have a shared vision, we must understand that the vision we have created is a guide, not a goal. The vision is what we aspire to, are continually working towards, reflecting on and adjusting. A vision allows us to continually assess what we are doing. A goal has an end point, and as we know, wellbeing has no end point.

To ensure the vision doesn't just stay as a lofty ambition that isn't realised, we have to be proactive in prioritising it and setting goals accordingly. When setting goals to support the vision, you may like staff to share everything they feel is getting in the way of achieving the vision, so the strategies and actions you devise support not just the goal, but the vision itself.

Another reason to create a vision is that a vision is limitless. It allows us to always expand and evolve, which is what is needed in the space of teacher wellbeing – and because schools themselves, including the curriculum, are continually changing. Underneath the vision, we can set aligned goals as needed, but the vision is the guide that keeps us on track. If all we do is set goals with no vision, it is likely that our goals will be disjointed and not allow us to achieve our desired state.

We have to come back to the question, 'How do staff at our school want to feel, act, think and be?'. When we answer these questions and allow staff to be a part of the process, we remove everything that is unrelated, and instead focus only on what supports wellbeing. If staff want to feel organised, have more time, feel more connected, have positive relationships, feel supported and calm and be more present for their students, your vision should support this.

Your vision and the supporting goals should also be a part of your school's strategic plan (or similar). If we are wanting to make teacher wellbeing a key focus in schools, building it into the school plan means the vision and goals created can more easily happen. This also supports the notion that teacher wellbeing is part of what we do and not an add-on or something we only do when we notice teachers are tired, stressed or overwhelmed. Your vision and supporting goals should aim to prevent ongoing reactive responses, and in return see teacher wellbeing as part of what you constantly do.

Utilising Staff Strengths

There is a lot to be said for supporting staff to work within their strengths, and it certainly can impact everyday and workplace wellbeing in the areas of meaning, fulfilment, growth and achievement, and purpose. By focusing on their strengths, teachers are more likely to be successful in their role.

It's no secret that some teachers are better at certain things than others. Some teachers are great at teaching early years, whereas others are better at teaching high school; some teachers excel at planning and the paperwork that goes with it, whereas others are better at resourcing and designing and coming up with ideas for amazing lessons; some teachers are better at using group work than others; and some teachers are experts with technology.

Knowing what our strengths are and how to utilise them is a strength in itself. Many of us have been told to set goals or focus on things that we aren't good at, and believe that growth can only come from seeing weaknesses and using a deficit approach. This is inaccurate. There are many benefits to focusing on our strengths. However, many of us don't recognise our strengths, partly because we have been told a strength is something we are good at – and if we aren't good at something it's not a strength and we should work on it.

There are several definitions of strengths that have now come to light in the space of positive psychology, and that can help us to better understand what it means to know and utilise our strengths. These definitions are different to those that appear in the dictionary, which centre around something being strong or weak. So, if a strength is more than just something we are good at, what is it?

According to positive psychology experts, there a few ways we can define strengths to help recognise what is a personal strength for ourselves. A strength may not always be present, but may require a trigger to bring it into action. It may support how we perform, energise us (or de-energise us if we overuse it), or be part of our natural ability to be near-perfect in performance consistently. Table 14 provides some definitions and characteristics of strengths.

Definition	Source
Attributes that support us to perform well or at our best.	Wood et al. 2011
A way of thinking, feeling and expressing emotions that leads to exceptional performance and can energise or strengthen us.	Brook and Brewerton 2006
The ability to produce consistent, near-perfect performance in an activity.	Buckingham and Clifton 2001
Can be latent until situations or experiences activate them.	Lyons and Linley 2008

Table 14: Definitions and Characteristics of Strengths
(Source: Adapted from Langly Group 2022)

Focusing on our strengths can make us more productive and happier in the workplace. Further, developing people's strengths has also been found to increase engagement and performance, while lowering attrition. It helps people to become more confident, productive and self-aware (Gallup 2022).

By focusing on strengths and supporting teachers to grow in specific areas, we can also positively influence school culture. The reason for this is that when we focus on our strengths, rather than our weaknesses, we are naturally doing something that energises and motivates us – hence we are in a more positive state, increasing positive emotions, making us more engaged in the workplace.

So how do we utilise our staff strengths? There are many tools and surveys you can use to identify and maximise staff strengths, so if you intend to focus on a strengths-based approach to building teacher wellbeing, I suggest you utilise a reputable, research-based tool and if possible engage someone trained or certified who can help you unpack it. Here are some steps to get you started:

- *Provide opportunities for staff to identify, learn about and reflect on their strengths.* As mentioned, use a consistent strengths-based tool with staff so they understand each other's strengths through shared language.
- *Find ways for staff to utilise their strengths.* Give staff opportunities to share their strengths and how they may be able to use these in the school setting; this could be as a teacher in their classroom, within their teams or across the school.
- *Think outside the box.* Moving to a strengths-based approach in your school setting may mean doing things differently. I know change in schools can be challenging, but to improve wellbeing things may have to be done differently – for example, collaborating and planning based on strengths rather than everyone doing the same thing. This may look like some teachers doing the written component and others making the resources rather than each teacher planning and resourcing individually.
- *Use a strengths-based approach to performance and feedback.* Instead of focusing on staff weaknesses, move to a strengths-based approach and set goals and targets based on strengths. By doing this you are also supporting staff to feel more engaged, fulfilled and energised by what they do each day.
- *Build a strengths network.* Often in schools we place expectations on staff or give them roles based on their job description or title without any thought to their strengths. A strengths network will allow you to consider the tasks that need doing, and assign people with the strengths needed to complete each task – rather than setting the task and having people try to match their strengths when perhaps they don't fit, or it de-energises them and causes them more stress. This will also require out-of-the-box thinking.

Having Strong Infrastructure

The infrastructure that surrounds how we do things in our schools – especially how teachers plan, work together, collaborate, mark, assess, and complete other tasks required in the teaching space that make up our professional responsibilities – is incredibly important. We need supportive systems, structures and processes to support teacher wellbeing and ensure we function properly.

At the school level, it really is the leaders' responsibility to make sure the infrastructure built is supportive. That means the systems, structures and processes in place for how teams work together, how planning is done, assessment schedules and cycles, entering data and so on sit at a school level. As leaders and decision-makers, we must be mindful to ensure the systems, processes and structures we put in place support teacher wellbeing and don't negatively impact it.

The infrastructure we use in a school is the way in which we do things. It covers just about everything you can think of that contributes to how we do our job:
- timetables
- lessons times and bell times
- playground duties
- planning templates for unit plans
- day planners
- assessment schedules
- meetings – team meetings, staff meetings and professional learning communities (PLCs)
- operational aspects of meetings; for example, agendas
- technology used for things such as role marking, data input and recording student behaviour
- how the school is organised on a daily basis
- communication platforms and procedures.

Like the infrastructure of a city – such as roads, buildings and communal areas – our school infrastructure may have initially been designed and built with the best intentions in mind, however, at times, may not serve the purpose it was designed for. We have all questioned how we can experience traffic jams on a newly opened road, or wonder why the public transport system never runs on time, or why some parks don't have any shade; the answer is, the infrastructure is letting us down. In a school, we need to review our infrastructure to make sure it is working as intended and that people aren't stuck in a traffic jam somewhere along the way. The only way to really know if the systems, structures and processes are supportive of teacher wellbeing is to ask our teachers.

We need to support teachers to be open to sharing what they feel is and isn't working, and in order to create the best way of doing things we need to include them in this process. Inviting teachers to share what negatively impacts their wellbeing will highlight gaps in how things are done. It could be that planning meetings are not being utilised because no one is managing how time is used. It could be that the day assembly is on isn't the best fit for how students show up to class. It could be that the assessment schedule and turnaround time for marking and data input is too tight and causing stress and overwhelm. It could be that there isn't a feedback and performance process so teachers don't know if or how they can grow.

What is highlighted will depend on what is a priority and what you may choose to focus on first. If feedback suggests our systems, structures and processes aren't working, then choosing to improve one at a time is the best way to tackle this – knowing that we can't change everything at once.

It's also important to note that while there may not be anything notably wrong, we can always be improving the way we are doing things. However, if things are going smoothly, and the systems, structures and processes are working, it does allow us more time to focus on other things.

That's the thing with infrastructure: if it is designed and built well, it helps everything within the organisation run smoothly and operate as intended – and you almost don't even realise it's there. The more smoothly things operate, the more efficient and productive we are, the more engaged we become, and the more school culture is positively influenced.

If the premise of school organisational infrastructure is to ensure teachers can perform well, operate effectively and efficiently, and to better systemise the processes and ways things are done, it is imperative for teacher wellbeing that this is an area of focus for schools.

All of the items in the list at the beginning of this section, and I am sure more, contribute to the infrastructure of the school and can affect teacher wellbeing. It is these things that need to be looked at and adapted if they are not allowing teachers to perform well and work productively and with ease, or if they are causing frustration, stress or adding to teachers' workloads.

I'm not saying we need to eliminate any of the above infrastructure – each piece is essential to how we work and operate as teachers. Rather, we need to ensure we are finding, implementing and using the most easeful, efficient and effective systems, structures and processes to support the infrastructure in our schools and support teacher wellbeing.

Fostering Flexibility

It may seem odd to suggest flexibility when the previous strategy focuses on having strong infrastructure, but what we know about wellbeing is that is not the same for everyone. As we begin to better support teacher wellbeing, we must allow for a certain degree of flexibility.

When we think of our students with varying needs, personalities, strengths, interests, backgrounds, experiences and circumstances, we are very careful to offer a flexible and supportive environment. This same way of thinking also needs to be applied to teachers.

A culture that allows for flexibility understands that it is the people we need to support, before the performance and outcomes we try to achieve. We cannot expect all teachers to be the same or need the same support. Instead, it is about looking at what staff need individually and collectively, and doing the best we can to support that.

This may mean focusing on different areas of everyday and/or workplace wellbeing and giving staff the autonomy to make decisions about what they feel they need to support their wellbeing. Autonomy is crucial as it allows for teachers to have the independence and freedom needed to make decisions for themselves. Autonomy means teachers get to have a say in what they need help with, what they want to improve or focus on, or suggest an area they are trying to strengthen and be given permission to work on that. This is important as those with more autonomy over their life have a higher sense of wellbeing.

We need to promote flexible approaches to supporting wellbeing. Not everyone needs to do a yoga class, not every teacher struggles with being productive and not every teacher lacks engagement in their role. Some teachers need more support and time to plan because they are learning to differentiate; some might need a later start one or two days a week because they have small children or care for elderly parents; some might need help getting organised because it isn't a strength of theirs. We are not all the same and do not need the same approach for our wellbeing. We need more flexibility in the approach our schools take.

So, what does it mean to be flexible in the workplace? According to the Fair Work Ombudsman (n.d.), 'Workplace flexibility means employers and employees making arrangements that suit them. This helps employees maintain their work/life balance and can improve business productivity and efficiency.'

If this is true, then again we need to think a little more outside the box when it comes to teacher wellbeing. If we want happier, more engaged teachers, who want to stay in the profession and feel rewarded, could being more flexible in how we do things be a somewhat simple solution, or at least part of a solution? The Fair Work Ombudsman (n.d.) also reports that while flexible working arrangements are a right of some employees, best practice employers are supporting all employees with flexible arrangements. It is said that while this supports the employee, it also creates happier, more motivated and committed staff, improves productivity, helps to attract skilled workers and reduces staff turnover. These sound like benefits all schools need.

To make things a little more complicated, there is no line that can be drawn between work and home, or that will allow work/life balance to be instantly achieved. Instead, we need to acknowledge that flexibility may be needed to best support the wellbeing of teachers and other staff. It's not common practice for schools to execute flexibility with work hours or time on site, especially because we are required to look after students each and every day; but I do wonder how a more flexible working environment would support teacher wellbeing, and what is possible?

For example, is it possible to allow teachers to start later one day a week – if not at a system level, what about an individual school level? Could teachers work from home if they weren't teaching at that moment during the day? Could we restructure timetables to allow teachers to work from home for half a day a week? Could teams who choose to meet early in the morning as opposed to staying late in the afternoon be offered the opportunity to do so? Could we have flexible start and finish times or compressed hours where possible?

I wonder about many things in this space, and I'm excited by the idea that flexibility could be one way, among others, to support teacher wellbeing. Perhaps it is time to think a bit more laterally. If we are still providing students with the best education possible, completing our work to a high standard, being accountable for the work we need to do and supporting each other to do so, is it possible that being flexible could positively influence teacher wellbeing? Could the idea of later starts, compressed hours, or meetings organised before school instead of after be one part of the solution to the complex issue that is teacher wellbeing?

The truth is, I don't know – but I have a feeling if we adopted flexibility, engaged staff and asked what this looks like for them, were creative in our approaches, worked together and supported one another, we could perhaps create a calmer, less stressful work environment where staff felt appreciated, valued and heard. This is not the entire answer, but it could be one piece of the puzzle, along with everything else in this chapter, and book.

Chapter Summary

- Schools can do a number of things to support teacher wellbeing.
- The five main areas to consider are: building positive relationships, setting a clear vision with supportive goals, utilising staff strengths, having strong infrastructure and fostering flexibility.
- All staff should be consulted when deciding what to focus on and change to support teacher wellbeing.
- It is important to look at what is impacting your desired state of wellbeing alongside how you would like it to be so you know what to change and focus on.
- It may be time to think outside the box and do things differently.

From Theory to Action

Let's take a look at some reflective questions for each of the strategies covered in this chapter.

Building Positive Relationships

Use the following questions to reflect on how you build positive relationships:
- Do you have opportunities to build positive relationships in your annual staff calendar?
- How could you do this more frequently?
- What time do you give to building positive relationships?
- Is it enough, do you need more, or is there too much?
- Do you find ways for staff to connect both personally and professionally?
- Do you provide opportunities for positive relationships to be strengthened in existing meetings?
- Do you have a balance of formal and informal ways to build positive relationships?

Setting a Clear Vision with Supportive Goals

Use the following questions to reflect on your teacher wellbeing vision:
- Is teacher wellbeing part of your school's strategic plan? If not, how could you prioritise this?
- Do you have a shared and collaborative vision for teacher wellbeing? If not, how could you create one?
- Have you given time to investigating and exploring what is impacting teacher wellbeing? If not, how could you do this?
- Do you have goals, targets and objectives to focus on to enhance teacher wellbeing? Are they aligned to your overarching vision? If not, how could you do this?

Utilising Staff Strengths

Using the five steps to maximising teacher strengths, reflect on how you do this in your school, and how you may be able to make this part of your teacher wellbeing strategy?
- Are opportunities provided for staff to identify, learn about and reflect on their strengths?
- Are ways for staff to utilise their strengths encouraged?
- Is it possible to think outside the box to support people to use their strengths?
- Is a strengths-based approach used to address performance and feedback?
- Is a strengths network utilised and are teachers supported to use this?

Having Strong Infrastructure

Consider the systems, structures and processes in your school. Do these support or impact teacher wellbeing? I highly encourage you to work with your staff to list everything that is part of your school infrastructure and to consider if each item is effective, efficient and being done as best it can, if it is positively or negatively impacting teacher wellbeing and if perhaps if it is time to review it adapt and/or change some of these things.

Fostering Flexibility

I just have one question for you – how could you create more flexibility in the way you do things to support teacher wellbeing?

Conclusion

Who knew the topic of teacher wellbeing would be so complex? In some ways, it has to be; if it were easy or simple, there would be one easy solution and it would be solved by now – but that isn't the case. What we can see and understand from the chapters before this is that teacher wellbeing is a complicated web of ideas, theory, art and science, research and studies, and trial and error, and that it looks different for every teacher, team and school. It is not linear, incremental, or something we can tick off a list and easily achieve; it is instead a complicated, messy road. This is aptly shown in figure 20 overleaf.

If only teacher wellbeing were a list of things to work through, achieve or do; if only it looked the same for everyone. However, as we know, that just isn't how it is. We have to be prepared to dive into the web, to begin to untangle it piece by piece, and at times get stuck along the way. That is just part of the wellbeing journey. You have to remember, wellbeing is about how we live, feel, be and are. Being human, is at times messy, complicated and predictable – so it makes sense that working on our wellbeing will be the same. I can attest however that while wellbeing does continually have its challenges, it gets significantly easier the more you work on it. As you build your own strategy, start to know what works and doesn't work for you, and are continually working on various wellbeing strategies day to day, it doesn't take as long or require as much effort to get back to your centre point, your point of equilibrium. You just have to continually do the work – even when it is hard, you feel like you don't want to, or it's easier to stay the same or go back to how it was before.

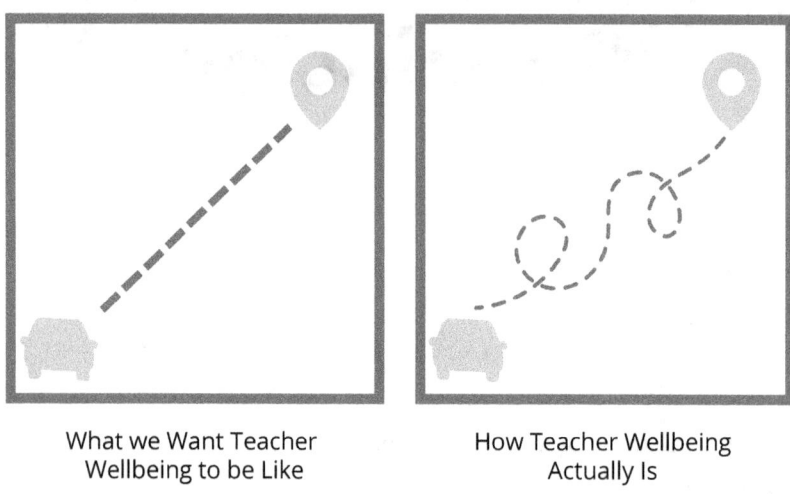

What we Want Teacher Wellbeing to be Like

How Teacher Wellbeing Actually Is

Figure 20: Working on Teacher Wellbeing – Expectation versus Reality

The strategies, focus areas and benefits of prioritising teacher wellbeing give us endless possibilities and options. What's more, we can layer and add on more strategies and approaches as needed. While at first this complicated web may not be easy to untangle or execute, I do think it can be done. What we need to understand, though, is that even though we'll have a deeper and more consistent understanding of teacher wellbeing through doing this work, this doesn't mean the approaches we take will be simple or consistent. I actually think this is great thing. If each teacher, team or school is working on something a little different, it shows they are doing what they need rather than what they think they should.

It is important to focus on individual needs and be data-informed when deciding what to concentrate on, but also be flexible. I was recently asked what the best data tool is to use when beginning this work; as I shared with the person who asked this question, the best data you can collect is the story that is being told. For you, this means tuning into how you feel, how you are spending your time and energy, what you feel and think is impacting your wellbeing, and what, if anything, you believe you can do about it. You may like to use the 'From Theory to Action' prompts in this book; reflect on each of the areas of the Teacher Wellbeing Framework; or just listen to what you are saying and thinking. By becoming aware of your thoughts and how you want to feel and be, you will have the best data you can have to help you know where to start.

If you are a leader or wanting to use this work in your school, talk to your staff and listen to what they say. Provide opportunities for everything to be shared, without judgement or immediate response, and use this data to inform where you are going to get the best return on investment for change. However, be prepared that where you think you need to start and what the data is telling you may be different. It may mean restructuring something in your school, improving a system around output, defining processes that are confusing or letting something go completely. Despite what we perceive the issue to be, the truth lies in the data. Part of improving teacher wellbeing and building positive culture means valuing your staff and their input, and using data like this is one important and essential way to do that.

Finally, I would like to end with this. Teacher wellbeing is the missing piece in school culture. Schools spend a significant amount of time, money and energy trying to improve school culture, but often neglect teacher wellbeing – and failing to see this as a piece of the puzzle or something worth focusing on. Culture is underpinned by the people in our organisations, and the better we look after our employees the better we serve our clients. Teachers are our employees; our students are our clients. If we look after our teachers, we will better serve our clients and everything that goes with that. This includes teaching, assessing, planning, teacher/student relationships, fostering engagement, how we work in teams and support school initiatives – it supports all of it. Improving culture happens when you value, support and work with your staff. This is the essence of teacher wellbeing.

References

Ackerman CE (2017) '23 Amazing Health Benefits of Mindfulness for Body and Brain', *PositivePsychology.com*. https://positivepsychology.com/benefits-of-mindfulness

Ackerman CE (2019) 'What is resilience and why is it important to bounce back?', *PositivePsychology.com*. https://positivepsychology.com/what-is-resilience/#resilience-definition

American Psychological Association (2020) 'Building your resilience'. https://www.apa.org/topics/resilience/building-your-resilience

Australian Curriculum, Assessment and Reporting Authority (ACARA; n.d.) *Health and Physical Education Glossary*. https://australiancurriculum.edu.au/f-10-curriculum/health-and-physical-education/glossary/?letter=W

Australian Institute for Teaching and School Leadership (AITSL; 2022) 'March 2022 Spotlight, Wellbeing in Australian Schools'. https://www.aitsl.edu.au/research/spotlights/wellbeing-in-australian-schools

Bandura A (1993) 'Perceived self-efficacy in cognitive development and functioning', *Educational Psychologist*, 28(2):117–148.

Be You/Beyond Blue (2022) 'Wellbeing'. https://beyou.edu.au/fact-sheets/wellbeing

Better Health Channel (2021) 'Wellbeing'. https://www.betterhealth.vic.gov.au/health/healthyliving/wellbeing

Bize R, Johnson J and Plotnikoff R (2007) 'Physical activity level and health-related quality of life in the general adult population: A systematic review', *Preventive Medicine*, 45:6.

Black Dog Institute (2022) 'Workplace wellbeing'. https://www.blackdoginstitute.org.au/resources-support/wellbeing/workplace-wellbeing/

Brook J and Brewerton P (2006) *Strengthscope Technical Manual*, Strengths Partnership.

Brown B (2015) *Rising Strong*, Penguin Random House.

Brown B (2021) *Atlas of the Heart: Mapping Meaningful Connection and the Language of Human Experience*, Penguin Random House.

Buckingham M and Clifton DO (2001), *Now, discover your strengths*, Free Press.

Cambridge University Press (2022) *Cambridge Dictionary*. https://dictionary.cambridge.org/dictionary/english/well-being

Celestine N (2021b) 'Supporting employee wellbeing in the workplace: 43 strategies', *PositivePsychology.com*. https://positivepsychology.com/employee-wellbeing/

Celestine N (2016) 'Broaden-and-Build Theory of Positive Emotions', *PositivePsychology.com*. https://positivepsychology.com/broaden-build-theory/

Celestine N (2021a) 'The Ryff scales of psychological wellbeing: your how-to guide', *PositivePsychology.com*. https://positivepsychology.com/ryff-scale-psychological-wellbeing

Chowdhury MR (2019) 'What is Emotional Regulation? + 6 Emotional Skills and Strategies', *PositivePsychology.com*. https://positivepsychology.com/emotion-regulation

Clear J (2018) *Atomic Habits: An Easy & Proven Way to Build Good Habits & Break Bad Ones*, Random House UK.

Collins (2022) *Collins Dictionary*. https://www.collinsdictionary.com

Covey S (2004) *The 7 Habits of Highly Effective People: Powerful Lessons in Personal Change*, Free Press.

David S (2021) 'Emotional Granularity Checklists'. https://www.susandavid.com/resource/emotional-checklist-general/

David S (2016) *Emotional Agility: Get Unstuck, Embrace Change and Thrive in Work and Life*, Avery Publishing House.

Davidson RJ (2019) 'How mindfulness changes the emotional life of our brains' [video], TED Talks. https://www.ted.com/talks/richard_j_davidson_how_mindfulness_changes_the_emotional_life_of_our_brains_jan_2019

Donohoo J, Hattie H and Eells R (2018) 'The Power of Collective Efficacy', ASCD. https://www.ascd.org/el/articles/the-power-of-collective-efficacy

Donohoo J (2016) *Collective Efficacy: How educators' beliefs impact student learning*, Corwin.

Edmondson A (n.d.) 'Psychological Safety'. https://amycedmondson.com/psychological-safety/

Encyclopedia Britannica (2022) *The Britannica Dictionary*. https://www.britannica.com/dictionary/resilience

Fair Work Ombudsman (n.d.) 'Workplace flexibility'. https://www.fairwork.gov.au/sites/default/files/minisite/static/3d21d6b6-7855-416c-bbe7-54e70762af68/workplace-flexibility/index.html

Fredrickson BL (1998) 'What Good Are Positive Emotions?', *Review of General Psychology*, 2(3):300–319.

Fredrickson BL (2004) 'The broaden-and-build theory of positive emotions', *Philosophical Transactions of the Royal Society B*, 359(1449).

Gallup (2022) 'Strengths development and coaching'. https://www.gallup.com/learning/248405/strengths-development-coaching.aspx

Geue PE (2018) 'Positive Practices in the Workplace: Impact on Team Climate, Work Engagement, and Task Performance', *The Journal of Applied Behavioural Science*, 54(3).

Goddard R and Salloum SJ (2012) 'Collective Efficacy Beliefs, Organizational Excellence, and Leadership', in Spreitzer GM and Cameron KS (eds) *The Oxford Handbook of Positive Organizational Scholarship*, Oxford University Press.

Goddard RD, Hoy WK and Hoy AW (2004) 'Collective Efficacy Beliefs: Theoretical Developments, Empirical Evidence, and Future Directions', *Educational Researcher*, 33(3).

Goleman D (2005) *Emotional Intelligence: Why It Can Matter More Than IQ*, Random House.

Heffernan A, Longmuir F, Bright D and Kim M (2019) *Perceptions of Teachers and Teaching in Australia*, Monash University. https://www.monash.edu/thank-your-teacher/docs/Perceptions-of-Teachers-and-Teaching-in-Australia-report-Nov-2019.pdf

Hersey P and Blanchard KH (1977) *Management of Organizational Behavior: Utilizing Human Resources*, Prentice Hall.

Isham A, Jackson T and Mair S (2019) *Wellbeing and productivity: a review of the literature*. https://www.researchgate.net/publication/338899227_Wellbeing_and_productivity_a_review_of_the_literature

Kahn WA (1990) 'Psychological Conditions of Personal Engagement and Disengagement at Work', *Academy of Management Journal*, 33(4):692.

Kids Help Line (2022) 'Building Resilience'. https://kidshelpline.com.au/teens/issues/building-resilience

Kose A (2016) 'The Relationship between Work Engagement Behavior and Perceived', *Journal of Education and Practice*, 7(27).

Langly Group (2022) 'Four strengths tools based on positive psychology'. https://langleygroup.com.au/four-strengths-tools-based-on-positive-psychology/

Learner Lab (n.d.) 'A Guide to Psychological Safety'. https://thelearnerlab.com/a-guide-to-psychological-safety/

Lyons LS and Linley PA (2008) 'Situational strengths: A strategic approach linking personal capability to corporate success', *Organisations and People*, 15: 4–11.

Moore C (2016) 'Albert Bandura: Self-Efficacy for Agentic Positive Psychology', *PositivePsychology.com*. https://positivepsychology.com/bandura-self-efficacy/

National Sleep Foundation (2020) 'What is REM Sleep?'. https://www.thensf.org/what-is-rem-sleep/#

Neff K (2022) 'Definition of Self-Compassion.' https://self-compassion.org/the-three-elements-of-self-compassion-2

Queensland Health (2019) 'Good mood food – how food influences mental wellbeing'. https://www.health.qld.gov.au/news-events/news/good-mood-food-how-food-influences-mental-wellbeing-anxiety-depression-stress

Riopel L (2019) 'Resilience skills, factors, and strategies of the resilient person', *PositivePsychology.com.* https://positivepsychology.com/resilience-skills

Robbins S and Judge T (2012) *Organizational Behavior.* Nobel.

Roozeboom MB and Schelvis R (2015) 'Work engagement: drivers and effects', http://oshwiki.eu/wiki/Work_engagement:_drivers_and_effects

Ryan RM and Deci EL (2001) 'On happiness and human potentials: A review of research on hedonic and eudaimonic well-being', *Annual Review of Psychology,* 52:141–66.

Ryff CD and Keyes CL (1995) 'The structure of psychological well-being revisited', *Journal of Personality and Social Psychology,* 69(4):719–27.

Seligman ME (2012) *Flourish: A visionary new understanding of happiness and well-being.* Atria Paperback.

Seligman ME and Csikszentmihalyi M (2000) 'Positive Psychology: An introduction', *American Psychologist,* 55(1):5–14.

Seligman ME, Parks AC and Steen T (2004) 'A Balanced Psychology and a Full Life', *Philosophical Transactions of the Royal Society B: Biological Sciences,* 359(1449): 1379–1381.

Selva J (2018) 'How to Set Healthy Boundaries: 10 examples + PDF Worksheets', *PositivePsychology.com.* https://positivepsychology.com/great-self-care-setting-healthy-boundaries/

Soong J (2022) 'What counts as water? Stay hydrated and healthy', Grow by WebMD. https://www.webmd.com/parenting/features/healthy-beverages

Stroud G (2017) 'Why do teachers leave?' ABC News. https://www.abc.net.au/news/2017-02-04/why-do-teachers-leave/8234054

Swaminathan N (2008) 'Why does the brain need so much power?', *Scientific American.* https://www.scientificamerican.com/article/why-does-the-brain-need-s/

Tillott S (2020) 'Adaptive and maladaptive traits of resilience', *Teacher.* https://www.teachermagazine.com/au_en/articles/adaptive-and-maladaptive-traits-of-resilience

Wilson R and Carabetta G (2022) 'Covid and schools: Australia is about to feel the full brunt of its teacher shortage', ABC News. https://www.abc.net.au/news/2022-01-19/covid-schools-australia-feel-brunt-teacher-shortage-omicron/100764472

Wood AM, Linley PA, Maltby J, Kashdan TB and Hurling R (2011) 'Using personal and psychological strengths leads to increases in well-being over time: A longitudinal study and the development of the strengths use questionnaire', *Personality and Individual Differences,* 50: 15–19.

World Health Organization (2022a) 'Constitution'. https://www.who.int/about/governance/constitution

World Health Organization (2022b) 'Health and Well-being'. https://www.who.int/data/gho/data/major-themes/health-and-well-being

Acknowledgements

There are so many people who have been crucial to helping me make it here – not just completing this book, but also allowing me to really and truly find my voice and step into this space.

Firstly, I want to thank my publisher Alicia Cohen. Without you believing I had something to share, this book would still be a bucket-list item instead of a real thing. This book has and will not only change my life, but the lives of so may other educators, and you have played a massive part in making that happen. Along with the team at Amba Press and everyone who worked behind the scenes, including Brooke Lyons, my editor, who helped to make this book what it is.

My wonderful partner Steven, thank you. Thank you for always having the belief that I could do this even when I thought I couldn't. Thank you for supporting me with your words, your encouragement and your interest, reading chapter after chapter and listening to my ideas and whiteboard presentations, even though I would often change my mind. Thank you for being my worst and best critic and helping me grow even when I didn't want you to, and thank you for taking up triathlon and spending countless hours a week training (even though I complain about it) so I could have the time, space and freedom to follow my dreams also.

Thank you to my beautiful siblings, Jenna, Jon and Adam, for always being interested, cheering me on and being proud of what I do. Thank you, Jenna, for always listening to me ramble on as I try to make sense of life; to Jon for being more stressed about my wordcount (or lack thereof) and deadline than I was; and to Adam for always making me laugh and asking questions that make me think.

Thank you to my wonderful friends who too have been cheering me on from the sidelines. Special thanks to Fiona and Lauren. Fiona, thank you for listening to me ramble, rant and rave, on an almost daily basis. I could not have done this (or pretty much anything else) without our morning check-ins. Thank you Lauren for always being there, through everything. Even when there are significant time periods between catch-ups, I know you will always be there.

Thank you to those who have been influential to my career. Most significantly Belinda and Sam: thank you both for mentoring me, holding space when I needed it and always making time for me. Thank you both for always having an open door to your office when we worked together and the numerous coffee catch-ups afterwards. The influence you have both had on my career is more than you will know.

Thank you to two of the most amazing women and coaches I know, Emily and Carly. Emily, you have helped me in so many ways, more than you will know. I honestly would not be who I am without your influence. Thank you, Carly, for teaching me business can be fun, easy and done my way, and helping me to become even more of who I am. You came into my life just at the right time. I will forever be grateful to you both.

Thank you to everyone who read this book in draft form and gave feedback. Special thanks to Selena Fisk for giving up so much of your time reading each and every word, fixing my typos and helping me to make this book even better.

Thank you to you, dear teacher, educator, leader and education supporter, for purchasing, reading and believing that this work matters.

About the Author

Amy Green is a leader and expert in improving culture and wellbeing for schools, organisations and individuals.

She is a published author, speaker, facilitator and coach who has a relatable approach to what can be a sensitive and personal topic. With a background in teaching, leadership and positive psychology, Amy brings a fresh take to this essential space.

Amy is dedicated to changing the way we view wellbeing in schools, empowering both leaders and educators to move from tokenistic, surface-level activities, to long-term, embedded, sustainable approaches. This means moving beyond morning teas and yoga classes to more strengthened, consistent strategies that focus on improving teacher wellbeing through building teacher capacity and enhancing school systems and processes. Amy's vision is to have schools across the globe making data-informed decisions that support teacher and staff wellbeing while building self and collective teacher efficacy.

Amy works with schools and educators in a variety of capacities, including:

- *School consultancy.* Through working as a critical friend to review what impacts teacher wellbeing in your school, Amy designs bespoke consultancy opportunities to your school on its teacher wellbeing journey. Amy carries out data collection allowing you to make informed decisions that make the work of teacher wellbeing relevant to your school. Amy works alongside principals, leadership teams, teaching teams and the whole staff through long-term consultancy, and provides professional development opportunities to enhance teacher and staff wellbeing.
- *Leadership and wellbeing coaching.* Amy uses a combination of various coaching strategies and methodologies, including positive psychology and her expertise as a teacher and leader to coach principals, leaders and teachers in the space of leadership and wellbeing.
- *Teacher wellbeing mentoring.* Amy runs an exclusive teacher mentoring program to help make teaching easier, more effective and more engaging for all teachers, supporting their wellbeing both in and out of the classroom.

To discuss how Amy can work with you or your school email:
hello@amygreen.com.au

Connect with Amy online:
www.thewellnessstrategy.com.au

LinkedIn: https://www.linkedin.com/in/amygreen/
Instagram: https://www.instagram.com/_thewellnessstrategy/
Facebook (group): https://www.facebook.com/groups/theteacherwellbeinghub
Facebook: https://www.facebook.com/thewellnessstrategy

www.ingramcontent.com/pod-product-compliance
Lightning Source LLC
Chambersburg PA
CBHW050022130526
44590CB00042B/1726